Practical Pre-School

GU01019210

The National Standards in Practice

by Liz Wilcock

Contents

Illustrated by Cathy Hughes

The views expressed in this book are those of the author.

Published by Step Forward Publishing Limited, The Coach House, Cross Road, Milverton, Leamington Spa CV32 5PB Tel: 01926 420046   www.practicalpreschool.com

Published in Great Britain © Step Forward Publishing Limited 2002

All rights reserved. No part of this publication may be reproduced, stored in a retrieval system, or transmitted by any means, electronic, mechanical, photocopied or otherwise, without the prior permission of the publisher.

The National Standards in Practice   ISBN 1-902438-77-9

Introduction

In September 2001, the Ofsted Early Years Directorate took responsibility for the registration and inspection of all day care providers and childminders. National Standards were introduced for under eights day care and childminding and guidance books were published to help all providers meet the standards.

The purpose of the National Standards is clear. They represent 'a baseline of quality below which no provider may fall'. They are also intended 'to underpin a continuous improvement in quality in all settings'. The National Standards will also ensure that the care of young children is consistent across the country so that no matter where the care is provided, the standards to be reached will be the same for each type of provider.

Previously, each local authority had issued their own standards for people providing day care, and they varied greatly across the country. Although they were based on guidance under the Children Act 1989, interpretations were different. This caused difficulties for some providers - for example, owners of several nurseries situated in different areas - who found that standards varied to such a degree that they could not be certain which set really reflected the requirements of the Children Act.

Ofsted inspections

Local authorities had the responsibility for registering and inspecting day care settings under Part X (10) of the Children Act 1989. This responsibility fell to Ofsted when the Care Standards Act 2000 amended the Children Act 1989 by adding a new Part Xa (10a) to regulate childminding and day care in England and Wales.

This now makes the roles of local authorities and Ofsted clearer. Local authorities keep responsibility for advice, support and training of all applicants and existing registered providers. Ofsted's responsibility is to regulate - their work involves dealing with new applications for registration, carrying out inspections, investigating complaints and taking enforcement action where necessary. This extends the responsibilities of Ofsted and is carried out within the new Early Years Directorate under the leadership of Maggie Smith as Director for Early Years.

This is a major change for Ofsted, who are mainly known for their educational inspections of primary and secondary schools. However, Ofsted does already carry out inspections in early years settings that receive a nursery grant to provide education for three- and four-year-olds. This means that some of you are used to being inspected by local authorities as well as Ofsted. Now, Ofsted Early Years will look at care as part of their work. Local authorities are no longer involved in the registration and inspection of early years settings.

Combined inspections

Providers who receive a nursery education grant will have combined inspections within agreed timescales. A combined inspection is one that combines the annual Children Act inspection with an inspection of funded nursery education under Section 122 of the School Standards and Framework Act. The main programme of combined inspections started in June 2002. Around 4,000 combined inspections are planned for each year. In many settings, one inspector will carry out the whole combined inspection. In some larger settings, two inspectors may work together. Combined inspections will take place once every four years unless the setting's provision has significant weaknesses in the funded educational programme, in which case they will be more often. In all other years between combined inspections, settings will have their usual annual Children Act inspection under the National Standards. The combined inspections will be carried out unannounced, like the Children Act inspections. Providers will know the month of the inspection, but not the exact date.

Standards and guidance

Childcare inspectors, many of whom previously worked within local authorities, are employed by Ofsted Early Years to inspect all day care provision under the National Standards. The standards reflect the current types of provision and can be identified by their colour:

Childminders - blue
Sessional groups - purple
Creches - green
Full day care - red
Out of school care - orange

Each standards book has accompanying guidance which has been produced by Ofsted to give applicants and registered providers a greater understanding of how to achieve the National Standards. The guidance books are colour coded in the same way as the standards books. These books are available to you through:

- your local Children's Information Service (CIS);

- your support/development teams in your Early Years Development and Childcare Partnership (EYDCP);

- DfES Publications, PO Box 5050, Sherwood Park, Annesley, Nottingham NG15 0DJ or visit the website at www.dfes.gov.uk/daycare or, for the guidance books only, go to www.ofsted.gov.uk and click on childcare.

How are the inspections organised?

England has been split into eight regions, each with its own regional centre:

■ **South West**
Regional centre - Bristol

■ **West Midlands**
Regional centre - Birmingham

■ **Eastern**
Regional centre - Harlow

■ **North East**
Regional centre - Leeds

■ **London**
Regional centre - London

■ **North West**
Regional centre - Manchester

■ **East Midlands**
Regional centre - Nottingham

■ **South East**
Regional centre - Woking

Each centre has a regional manager, area managers and senior childcare inspectors, who oversee the inspection work carried out by the childcare inspectors.

The inspection teams

In each centre there are teams of people with different responsibilities. The administrative staff will help you through the process of applying to register as an early years provider. The National Helpline phone number (0845 601 4771) will take you through to your regional centre. This number is also for general enquiries.

Always make a note of the date you have called, the purpose of your call, and record the name of the person you have spoken to. This means that you can ask for the same person again, and not have to go over information each time you call. Put things in writing as well - and keep a copy. This will enable you to keep track of what was sent, and when, in case there are any delays. The message is this - keep the administration team informed, both verbally and in writing, and try to be patient.

Every area has about eight to ten childcare inspectors (CCIs) who are line managed by a senior childcare inspector (SCCI). The CCIs work from home. This has been difficult for some providers, who had previously had regular contact with the team responsible for registration and/or inspection. These teams were called under eights officers/day care advisers. Most local authorities had the same team of people carrying out registrations and inspections, in addition to investigating complaints and being responsible for enforcement.

Many of the CCIs now employed by Ofsted are still working in the areas they had worked in previously as under eights officers/day care advisers. However, their approach to your inspections will be different. Appointments will not usually

be made for your inspections now. You will be advised only of the month that your annual inspection will take place. Providers, especially childminders, will get the opportunity to tell Ofsted of any commitments. Childminders are not expected to stay in every day for a whole month!

The point of contact for you now, should you have problems or need advice, is the local development/support team in your EYDCP. If you have not had contact with your local support worker yet, it is worth

making a call to your local education department for early years, who will put you in touch with someone. The Children's Information Service in your area is responsible for holding the lists of registered providers. The information is passed on from Ofsted Early Years when settings/childminders are first registered. It is worthwhile contacting your local Children's Information Service to check what details they have about you, as they are available to parents looking for childcare.

The complaints, investigation and enforcement team has a specific role in relation to early years settings. The team will advise and give support to inspectors and providers on investigation and enforcement issues.

When complaints are made about a provider, obviously some action needs to be taken. It is likely that your transitional inspection will take place at an earlier time than planned by the inspection team. Your transitional inspection is called this because it is your first inspection under Ofsted Early Years. (Until you have this inspection, you need to make sure that you are complying with all the conditions stated on your current certificate. Some providers have been concerned as the date has expired on their current certificate, and they think that they may be operating illegally. This is not the case.) If a complaint is made about you, your inspection may be brought forward, so that the issues can be raised with you. Following your transitional inspection, you will be inspected under the National Standards every year.

The National Standards

As a parent, what would you want to know about your child when they were being cared for by someone else? It is likely that their safety and well-being would be at the top of your list, followed by the opportunities for them to mix with other children, develop their social skills, and enjoy activities that will enable them to develop to their potential. These are the underlying principles for the National Standards.

There are 14 National Standards that apply to all day care settings, including childminders. The inspectors will want to know how you will meet all 14 standards. They are:

■ Suitable person

■ Organisation

■ Care, learning and play

■ Physical environment

■ Equipment

■ Safety

■ Health

■ Food and drink

■ Equal opportunities

■ Special needs

■ Behaviour

■ Partnership with parents

■ Child protection

■ Documentation

There are annexes at the end of the standards for providers to consider the criteria for:

■ Caring for children under two

■ Overnight care

These are considered at the end of this book (see pages 63-64).

Ofsted's inspectors will, through questions and observations, judge whether you meet the National Standards. Your inspection will be outcome based, in other words, the CCI will want to establish how you meet the standards. The questions they ask will be open-ended, meaning that you will need to respond with explanations. For example, the inspector may ask you 'How do you meet the needs of all the children who attend, in terms of their diet?' You

need to be prepared for this by providing menus that reflect the cultural and special dietary needs of the children, and by explaining your understanding of the importance of offering a balanced nutritional diet. Evidence to show how you reach each of the 14 standards can be provided in two ways - verbally, and through your documentation, such as your policies and procedures.

What do you need to know?

Many providers believe that they will be expected to show/achieve *everything* in the standards. The actual standard to be achieved is written in bold print under the heading of each standard. For example, Standard 11 (Behaviour):

Adults caring for children in the provision are able to manage a wide range of children's behaviour in a way which promotes their welfare and development.

Under the heading, there are supporting criteria for you to *give consideration to*. For example, 11.1 - 11.6 are points for you to consider to enable you to meet Standard 11, but how you meet the standard is up to you. Ofsted has given you more details in the guidance books that support the standards.

Under Standard 11 (Behaviour), for example, you can:

11.1 – consider writing a behaviour statement

11.2 - think about how you will encourage positive behaviour

11.3, 11.6 - recognise the importance of the role of the adult

11.4, 11.5 - agree with all staff on a consistent approach to managing children's unacceptable behaviour.

The important sections in the guidance books under each standard are in the boxed information, headed 'Children Act Regulations'. For example, under Standard 4 (Physical environment), the guidance book states that you must notify Ofsted if any changes are made to the premises or their use.

There are no Children Act regulations for you to address under Standard 11.

Any boxed information in the guidance books that is related to the Children Act

regulations *must* be addressed. The inspector will ask how you meet all of the standards, giving regard to the criteria, but also complying with the requirements of the Children Act 1989.

Remember, your local support worker can give you help and advice in meeting this and all of the standards.

How this book can help you

The purpose of this book is to consider in detail each of the 14 National Standards and how you can apply the information from the guidance books to your own circumstances, whether you work in a group setting or are a registered childminder, caring for children in your own home. You can use it alongside the National Standards document and your guidance book - all three books should complement each other.

Each of the standards will be considered in turn. The standard to be reached, and any specific requirements of the Children Act, will be clearly shown. The following points will be covered under each standard:

■ What does this mean for your setting?

■ What do you need to do?

■ Dealing with dilemmas

■ Good practice

■ What will the inspector be looking for?

Working together

The National Standards were produced by the DfES, and Ofsted Early Years Directorate were responsible for issuing the guidance books to support the standards document. EYDCP support staff work closely with Ofsted Early Years to raise issues on behalf of providers. In this way, things will move on to the benefit of all providers and the children in their care.

The National Care Standards are due to be reviewed in 2003, when the transitional period ends. The process for the review is yet to be decided. However, it seems likely that there will be no major changes.

Suitable person

The standard to be reached:
Adults providing day care, looking after children or having unsupervised access to them are suitable to do so.

Requirement that you must comply with: Children Act regulations
You must tell Ofsted about any changes to the person in charge or to adults living or employed on your premises. You must also inform Ofsted about any matter that might affect their suitability.

What does this mean for your setting?

What does the term 'suitable person' mean? You need to consider criteria points 1.1 - 1.4.

The registered person/people (this could be an owner of a setting, or a committee of a pre-school or out-of-school club) is responsible for ensuring that all conditions of registration are complied with at all times. Ofsted will satisfy themselves that the registered person is suitable, by taking up checks and references on the person/committee. These checks will also include health and police clearance. Ofsted leaves the responsibility for suitability of other staff employed by the setting to the registered person. This involves far more than just a police check, which so many providers think is the important check.

What do you need to do?

Your initial views on any person are formed when you first meet. However, you will be determining the person's suitability in a number of ways:

■ The interview

■ The person's CV (Full information should be available so that you can be sure you have all the details of work history, with no gaps.)

■ Qualifications

■ Age and experience

■ Health declaration

■ Police clearance

When staff are being recruited, the registered person has a responsibility to make sure that the staff are suitable. Look at your recruitment procedures. Do they reflect how you take on new staff? Do your application forms state clearly the post that is being applied for, with a full and clear job description? Does the wording in your advertisements allow for equality of opportunity? Do you have an induction package for new staff, so that they are aware of all of your policies and procedures?

The terms for employment (contract) for any new member of staff should be clear. As well as the place of employment and job title, you should state the pay conditions, hours of work and notice period. Be clear about sickness pay and holiday entitlements, in addition to clear disciplinary and grievance procedures. If a probationary period is offered, you should provide a contract to reflect this, with a permanent contract offered at the end of that time. Even if the position is temporary, a contract is advisable.

A contract and induction package means

that any new member of staff will be clear about their individual role and job responsibility. The contract will need to be signed as an agreement, and it is advisable to ask the new staff member to sign their name to the information given to them in the induction package, as a record that they have read it, understood and agree to follow the policies and procedures. Some settings issue the induction package to all staff as it is updated, so that everyone is in agreement on a consistent approach to the policies.

Employment issues are important, and most settings need advice at some stage on how to deal with specific queries. Your local support worker will be able to help you. You may also contact the Advisory, Conciliation and Arbitration Service (ACAS). ACAS has up-to-date information about current legislation that you need to know about.

You also need to think about other people working in your setting, such as those on work experience or volunteers,

Advisory, Conciliation and Arbitration Service (ACAS)
27 Wilton Street
London SW16 4ER
Tel: 0208 679 8000

Helpful publications
Recruiting Child Care Workers - A Guide for Providers - code EYDC PREP 5

Developing Child Care for Older Children and Young People - code EYDC PREP 3

Both available from DfES Publications. Ring them on 0845 6022260 or email dfes@prolog.uk.com

Smile and the world smiles with you.

to make sure that they are fully supported while they are with you.

Police checks are taken up through the Criminal Records Bureau (CRB). You will need to ask a new member of staff to complete a DC2 form. You can obtain these from Ofsted Early Years, and they can be photocopied. The DC2 form is for Ofsted's information. The CRB will also need to be contacted about each individual check, and you will need to quote the Ofsted number each time (20096400008). The CRB's telephone number is 0870 9090811.

Health checks are rather more difficult. Previously, the under eights officers/day care advisers dealt with the health checks for you, and advised you on the outcome of these, as well as the police checks. Now, you as the responsible person need to address this yourself. How are you going to satisfy yourself that the people you employ are 'fit' and suitable for the job? This has caused some anxiety among owners and committees. One suggestion is to devise your own health declaration form. New staff, and even existing staff, could declare every year that they are in good health. Your disciplinary procedures could come into force if you then had cause to question the signed declaration.

Taking up references is very important - preferably in writing. This will show that you have taken every opportunity to check out your staff. Part of your recruitment procedure should show that you offer positions for a probationary period, during which time you should try to get to know the new staff member, and offer support as the probationary time goes by. If, at the end of this time, you are happy with the person, you may choose to offer a permanent post. However, if things have not worked out, you may decide to either extend the probationary period, or tell the person that you will not be able to offer them a permanent post.

Ofsted Early Years Directorate will do some checks for you, on the people you employ. You need to advise your regional centre of any staff changes, and new staff will be checked against:

- The Protection of Children Act list

- DfES list 99

- Social services records

If you employ a person to manage your setting, you need to be certain that they are suitable before you leave them in charge. It is your responsibility to make sure that, in your absence, the setting is in good hands. This is more than just a qualification issue. They must be competent in their work and be able to demonstrate a clear understanding of the National Standards. Suitable qualifications for a person in charge are:

- Diploma in Nursery Nursing (NNEB)

Dealing with dilemmas

You are expanding your provision, and looking to recruit more staff. You have advertised locally for a qualified person (NNEB or similar), and a nursery assistant, who will be unqualified.

A friend's daughter contacts you for the position of nursery assistant, thinking that the job is a certainty, as you know her and the family so well.

Her manner with you is very informal, and you can tell that she has an expectation that you will just employ her on the basis that you know one another.

What are you going to do?

1. Be very clear - whoever applies for any position in your setting must complete an application form, giving details of people that can be contacted for references. These must not be family members, and should have known the applicant for at least three years.

2. All references need to be taken up, including police checks. Health, too, will need to be satisfactory (you may know personally of health issues for this person, however, it is for the person to inform you of any health matter that may affect their suitability). This could be sensitive, and therefore demonstrates why it is so important that you follow your recruitment procedures for all applicants equally.

3. You are unable to offer a job to someone on the basis that you know them. This would not be appropriate, and could be difficult for both of you.

4. The interview (if you offer one) must be arranged as for anyone else who has applied. You will not be the only person interviewing. The job offered is a professional post, and you need to conduct your interview in a professional but friendly way.

- B Tec National Diploma/Certificate in Early Childhood Studies

- NVQ Level 3 in Childcare and Education

- Pre-school Learning Alliance Diploma in Pre-school Practice

- Teaching Certificate

- Qualified Teacher Status (QTS)

- Health Visiting Certificate

- Appropriate level 3 social work qualifications

- Appropriate level 3 nursing qualifications

Qualifications alone, without appropriate experience, skills and ability, are not sufficient for a person in charge.

The person in charge may be nominated by the registered person to be available for the inspection with Ofsted Early Years.

• • • • • • • • • • • • • • • • • •

You may get additional information from the National Training Organisation on 01727 738300.

• • • • • • • • • • • • • • • • • •

Good practice

- Look at your setting now. You are likely already to be providing child care and education to a high standard. You are becoming familiar with the National Standards, and although you are comfortable with your preparation for Standard 1, are there some areas that you would like to show the inspector as being good practice?

Consider:

Recruitment - your paperwork, and how it is presented

- Do you keep your files for staff in a secure cabinet, where each member of staff has their own folder?

- Do you clearly show your recruitment procedures, and how you make the decisions on each appointment? What questions did you ask at interview to enable you to reach the decision?

- Do you show your support for the person in charge and all staff, through regular supervision and appraisal? Are the papers connected to these all available on each person's file?

You may have other examples of good practice such as:

- How often staff meetings are held, and the lines of communication between management and workers in your setting.

- How you approach training issues, and guide staff towards updating their knowledge.

These last two points are important if you are to remember about the monitoring of staff, following their appointment to work in your setting. Standard 1 is about the suitability of the people you employ and retain as staff.

What will the inspector be looking for?

Your guidance books, which were written by Ofsted Early Years, advise you at the end of each section about 'What the inspector looks for'. This is helpful as a checklist for you.

The records you hold about your staff, volunteers and students - *written evidence*

Your procedures for appointing new staff - *written and verbal evidence*

Your procedures for ensuring supervision of volunteers and students - *written evidence*

Any certificates of training or qualifications - *visual evidence*

Any changes to your circumstances since the last inspection - *verbal discussion*

The standard to be reached:
Adults providing day care, looking after children or having unsupervised access to them are suitable to do so.

Requirement that you must comply with:
Children Act regulations
You must inform Ofsted about any changes to your personal circumstances or to adults living or working on your premises. You must also inform Ofsted about any matter that might affect their suitability.

What does the term 'suitable person' mean? You need to consider criteria points 1.1 - 1.6.

A registered childminder cares for other people's children in his or her own home, for reward, usually financial payment. Unlike group care, a childminder normally works alone, caring for up to six children aged nought to eight. Members of the childminder's home may have access to the minded children, as well as visitors, so there is a responsibility placed on the individual childminder to have every consideration for children in their care.

When a child care inspector assesses you for suitability, there will be specific issues addressed. These are likely to include:

■ Your understanding of the 14 National Standards, and how you will apply them to your home environment.

It is likely that you will be able to say that you have attended a registration course through your local authority, that covered the National Standards, and show your attendance certificate.

■ Your situation regarding first aid training.

Most people wishing to register as childminders recognise the need for first aid training, and will have completed a recognised course before their inspection. Again, you can produce your certificate.

■ Other people in your home, and employed assistants.

Anyone over the age of 16 years will need to have completed a police check form for the Criminal Records Bureau (CRB). They are contactable on 0870 9090811. You need to quote the Ofsted number 20096400008. This will have been done before your inspection. The health and suitability of other people is for you to determine, and this may be more difficult in terms of health checks, due to confidentiality. You may decide to ask your assistant to declare that he/she is in good health. This is a sensitive issue, and you may want to ask your local support worker for help with this.

When the inspector talks to you about your work as a childminder, you will also need to think about the following:

■ What arrangements you have in place to protect the children from people who visit your home who are not vetted.

You should never leave the children unattended with visitors to your home, or anyone who has not been checked as being suitable.

■ How you will appoint an assistant.

Think about the person's suitability, in terms of knowledge and understanding of young children. Are they qualified? Look at any certificates and ask for copies. Take up references. Unless the assistant becomes registered in their own right, they should not be left unattended with the children. This may cause you some problems, as the children may be in different areas of your home - how will you deal with this? Consider asking your assistant to become registered.

Organisation

The standard to be reached:
The registered person meets the required adult:child ratios, ensures that training and qualifications requirements are met and organises space and resources to meet children's needs effectively.

Requirements that you must comply with: Children Act regulations
You must have procedures to be followed in the event of a child being lost or a parent failing to collect a child.

You must keep on the premises the name, address and telephone number of yourself, staff members, anyone living or employed on the premises, and any other person who will regularly be in unsupervised contact with the children.

What does this mean for your setting?

The key to this standard is effective planning. When you are thinking about ratios, staff deployment and contingency arrangements, you have a number of issues to consider. You, as a registered provider, will not be able to do this alone. A team effort is needed, with everyone connected to the setting involved. Your responsibility is to know what the requirements for the standard are, and then to work with the person in charge and staff to ensure that they are met.

Your main objective must be to make sure that the children are being cared for in a safe environment, and that the staff are with the children at all times, overseeing the welfare of each child. You will have satisfied yourself that all your staff are suitable through the requirements of Standard 1. However, you are still responsible for the monitoring of staff, either yourself, or through your manager/supervisor. You also need to be satisfied that on becoming employed in your setting, new members of staff agree to further training. Under this standard, *how* you put together an action plan of training for each member of staff will be looked at by the inspector. How will you do this?

Each member of staff should have their own training programme, stating current qualifications and what training is

proposed next. Timings for this could be agreed at appraisal, once a year, so training could be planned for the year, depending on which course(s) are discussed and agreed. It is your responsibility to ensure that all staff are adequately trained for the purpose of caring for young children. Your EYDCP will have a training programme/book for you and the staff to consider, and some have a training co-ordinator who can advise you on the appropriate training for staff in your setting.

What do you need to do?

Deployment of all staff/people on site needs careful consideration. In some settings, staff are responsible for cleaning the premises as well as caring for the children - this should not interfere with the care of the children. The main cleaning tasks should be carried out when the children are not on the premises, with general everyday tasks carried out in minimum time.

You should be aware at all times of any people on the premises, such as administration staff and students. If your setting is in a multi-use building all staff should be aware that other people are in the area who are not necessarily checked for work with young children. Staff must be vigilant at all times.

The manager of your setting may be supernumerary, employed over and above the staff who are directly working

with the children in terms of staff ratios. The manager or deputy should always be available, with the deputy able to take full charge in the absence of the manager.

Although the standard printed in bold does not actually state the ratios of staff:children, the criteria (2.7) is there as a guide for you, depending on the ages of the children in your setting. The ratios are as follows:

- One member of staff to three children aged between nought and two years

- One member of staff to four children aged between two years and three years

- One member of staff to eight children aged between three years and seven years 11 months

These are the minimum you work towards. Children over the age of eight, but under 14 years of age, will be considered too, in respect of the impact of their attendance on the younger children.

- Will you be able to meet the needs of all?

- Do you consider the areas for play to allow children free movement?

- Have you given thought to the layout of your premises to ensure that all children can access toilet facilities, and that staff can use nappy changing facilities near to the areas in which babies are being cared for? If staff have to walk some distance to either take the children to the toilet, or to change nappies, ratios may be affected, so this is worth considering.

You need to think about your staff deployment - the inspector will ask you about this. Consider where the qualified staff are based - there should always be one qualified member of staff in each room/area, supported by others who are undertaking training or who are unqualified. Anyone who has not gained a qualification to supervisory level, that is NNEB or NVQ 3, should not be left in charge of children in your setting. NVQ 2 qualified people are included in your 50 per cent of qualified staff, but do not hold a supervisory qualification. The person in charge of the babies should ideally have some experience, in addition to the qualification. The inspector will discuss qualifications of all staff at your inspection, and how your 50 per cent of staff with a qualification are deployed in your setting. The inspector will observe the staff with the children to see how everything works in practice, and will comment on the structure of the day, and how all the children's needs are being met.

Do you have arrangements in place to cover unexpected staff absences? These would be described as your contingency arrangements. Ofsted will expect an explanation if your ratios are not able to be met. You will need to have enough staff members to care effectively for all of the children in your setting. Always inform Ofsted of any staffing difficulties.

If the children are to go on an outing, you need to plan ahead. An outing may be a walk to the local shops or park, or a day out by coach to a farm, for example. Consider the following:

- Do you have the parents' permission in writing to take their children off the premises?
- What risks could there be for children, depending on their ages?
- Are you using a reputable coach company - seat belts, insurance and so on?
- Food and drink
- First aid kit and individual medication

Do you operate a key worker system, where a member of staff is responsible for a small group of children, speaking to the parents about the children's day and keeping the records of that group? Some settings do, others do not. The issue for your inspection is how all the children are to be cared for, who speaks to the parents, and how records are maintained. This is up to you and your setting. The inspector may ask 'How do you make sure that the needs of all the children are being met in terms of their

development?' You will need to answer this question clearly, showing the inspector the paperwork used by staff, and how all children are helped to progress in all areas of development.

What sort of paperwork will the inspector be looking for? Each child should have their own development records, which staff are responsible for keeping up to date. The records should show progress from the time the child started in your setting. The time it takes to complete these records is always an issue for staff - time which they would rather spend with the children. This is a matter that each setting needs to address, so that staff can have the time they need to observe and record details about the children in their care, without disruption to the routine of all of the children.

If you need advice on how key worker systems operate, or what alternatives there are, your support worker should be able to help.

The key to effective staffing is consistency, and how you employ and retain your staff is an issue for you to consider. Staff who feel appreciated and rewarded, valued and listened to, are more likely to stay in your setting. It is worth taking every opportunity to speak to the staff about how they are, and letting them know that if they need to discuss anything, you will be available. Child care is not usually well financially rewarded, so any words of thanks and praise are gratefully received. It is important for everyone who works in the setting to feel that they are a part of a team, and that their opinions matter. This is especially important when you come to look at your operational plan.

What is an operational plan?
This is a document/collection of documents that should be made available to parents. There should be several parts to the operational plan, and staff input is important if the plan is to work. How can you achieve this?

Arrange a meeting between all staff and yourself, allowing time to discuss the content of the operational plan, and then how it will be presented. It is likely that you already have something in place.

You may not be calling it your operational plan, but some of the points listed below will more than likely be within the working day of your setting:

- **Your premises, and the resources you have.** Resources means staff as well as play equipment. In your entrance area, do you have a staff photo board, identifying who is in charge, and all other staff, with their names, rooms they work in, and what qualifications they hold? A basic map, showing the layout of the premises?

- **Resources, in terms of play equipment.** What is available for each age group, to ensure that each child will have the opportunity to develop to his/her full potential? Where are all the resources stored, and do all staff know what is available? One person could be made responsible for holding an inventory of play materials/equipment. This would enable you to be kept informed of new items that need purchasing, and broken items that need replacing. A similar system could be put in place for nursery equipment/furniture, with you being kept informed.

- **Commitment to staff and their ongoing training.** The staffing structure should be made clear - who works where, and what their responsibilities are in the setting. Do remember everyone who works for you - kitchen help, cleaning staff and so on. How are the staff managed? Do you have regular supervision and annual appraisals in place? If not, this is something you need to consider, to show how you value your staff and how you intend to support them in their chosen career. Your support worker can advise you on how to get training yourself to do supervision and appraisals.

- **Your aims and objectives, policies and procedures.** Many settings have booklets/information sheets about their setting to give parents who are looking for child care the relevant information. This would normally include a general background, aims and objectives, booking procedures, charges, who to contact and so on. The parents who choose to send their child to your setting should have access to, or a copy of, all of your policies and procedures. If the staff have had input to these documents they will have some sense of ownership.

■ **Feedback from parents and others.** This is important, as it is a way in which you can consider what needs to be looked at again, and make changes. One way to do this is to have a visitors' book for everyone to sign, with dates, times and a space for comments, or parents may use a post box. Whatever you decide to do, remember, it is always best to be available to speak to anyone who wants to make a comment about your setting.

The visitors' book has another purpose - you should always know who is in the building for evacuation purposes. The visitors' book, alongside your registers, which show the staff and children present on that day, will be needed to account for everyone as they leave the building in case of a fire. The registers are important for a number of reasons:

1. They are a requirement of the Children Act.

2. Everyone's details will be recorded in one book - if you had to evacuate the premises due to a fire, you would be able to contact parents/next of kin from information held in one book.

3. A record of arrivals and departure times makes sure that you know exactly who is on the premises at any time, including visitors.

4. Special medical needs can also be recorded.

The register(s) should be kept in one place and taken out of the building at the end of each day/session/evacuation. Because of the confidential information held in the register, a secure place for storage should be found.

The guidance book states that the 'operational plan need not be a single document but can be a collection of policies and procedures. Review and update your plan to reflect the changing needs of staff and children'. What

policies and procedures do you need? Broadly, they come under five headings:

■ Health and safety
■ Equal opportunity
■ Child protection
■ Parents as partners
■ Management and administration

The policies and procedures will be individual to your setting. Under Standard 14 (Documentation), you will need to produce your policies and procedures for the inspector. (You will find more information later in this book under Standard 14 to help you with this.)

Good practice

■ Look at your organisation now. It is likely that you have staff that understand their roles and responsibilities. Children are being well cared for by staff, who recognise the importance of meeting each child's individual needs. How can you demonstrate good practice to the inspector under Standard 2?

Consider:

The visual evidence

■ The inspector will be observing the staff with children to assess how they meet the children's needs.

■ The inspector will note how the staff are deployed, and how they manage the structure of the day. If a child has an accident, and one member of staff takes the child to the toilet, how do the remaining staff members care for the rest of the children for that time?

■ Do you value the input of work experience pupils/students in your setting to make them feel a part of your setting whilst they are with you? What support do you offer?

What will the inspector be looking for?

Your operational plan and procedures - *visual evidence and discussion*

Where and how staff records are stored - *visual evidence*

Attendance registers for children and staff - *visual evidence*

Dealing with dilemmas

You have arranged an outing to the local park today for a picnic lunch and outdoor play. The staff:child ratios are no problem, and every parent has given written consent to their child going out today. You have a first aid kit, and all the food and drink is ready in cool boxes. Then a member of staff phones to let you know that she has been unwell overnight, and will not be able to come to work today. As your conversation ends, another member of staff tells you that she is feeling unwell, and may have to go home. You have a dilemma - you will not have enough staff to look after the children on your outing. What are you going to do?

Your options are:
1. Cancel the outing - safety measure

2. Ask parents if they can help - you may have enough adults, but ratios will be affected.

What must you do?
1. You must notify Ofsted of your staffing situation, as ratios, whether your outing takes place or not, are affected.

2. If you do not have enough staff to care adequately for all of the children, you may need to contact parents to collect their children. This is a part of your risk assessment, when you need to weigh up all the options, and make a decision.

It is likely that the outing will not take place today. The children will be disappointed. If the adult:child ratio can be maintained in the setting, the children could still have their picnic - indoors or in the pre-school garden - with fun games organised, so that the children still have a special time to remember.

Standard 2
Childminding

The standard to be reached:
The registered person meets required adult:child ratios, ensures that training and qualifications requirements are met and organises space and resources to meet the children's needs effectively.

Requirement that you must comply with: Children Act regulations
You must keep on the premises the name, address and telephone number of yourself, staff members, anyone living or employed on the premises, and any other person who will regularly be in unsupervised contact with children looked after there.

As a registered childminder, the number of children you can care for at any one time will have been agreed at your initial inspection, with the space in your home given consideration, as well as the numbers you hope to be able to care for. When a child care inspector visits you, there will be issues under Standard 2 that you will need to consider. These will be:

■ Any changes to your home circumstances that could affect your childminding.

You should keep Ofsted informed of any changes, such as a health matter that could affect your work, or changes to the premises in respect of building work. At your inspection you may wish to discuss numbers of children with your inspector - you may have decided to care for older children only, and would therefore not need to provide the range of equipment for younger children.

■ If you have an assistant working with you.

The inspector will want to know how you are planning your work with the assistant, and how the routine is managed. You will have discussed health and safety issues with your assistant, and be able to guide them in their work in your home.

■ Overnight care of minded children.

Some childminders have arrangements in place for this. You will need to demonstrate to the inspector how you manage overnight care in respect of

sleeping, bath time, contact with parents and so on. Your local support worker can talk through these issues with you on an individual basis

■ Attendance records and play space available for all children.

You should have some form of register/diary to show the details of the children you care for to show the inspector. Your home should be open for the inspector to see where you allow the children to eat, sleep and play, and you should be able to discuss how you plan your day. Your registration course should have prepared you well for this.

Care, learning and play

The standard to be reached:
The registered person meets children's individual needs and promotes their welfare. They plan and provide activities and play opportunities to develop children's emotional, physical, social and intellectual capabilities.

What does this mean for your setting?

The above statement is the standard you will be required to meet. Criteria points 3.1 - 3.9 cover the following:

■ Building positive relationships and developing self-esteem
■ Learning right from wrong
■ Learning and play opportunities
■ Language and mathematical thinking
■ Imagination and creativity
■ Planning and recording
■ Organising resources
■ Early Learning Goals

How will you achieve this standard with the range of age groups and abilities in your setting? Adults working with young children have a responsibility to ensure that all children are being cared for appropriately, in a safe environment. They should provide opportunities through play for children to develop to their potential. You may be working in a setting where children aged nought to five years are cared for, or in a pre-school, or be a childminder looking after up to six children aged between nought to eight, or looking after older children in an after-school club.Whatever your job, the key to this standard is planning, and keeping developmental records for each individual child.

Record keeping is vital if children's progress is to be monitored. Staff should have a system in place for keeping developmental records, so knowledge of child development is necessary. Regular observations of all children, either as they work in a group, or individually, are important, so that all significant

developments can be noted. This is important for every child, but even more so for children who are receiving additional support, as the smallest progress could be a major step for them.

Observing children does take time, and many carers are concerned about the time it takes to carry out their observations and keep the records up to date. This applies to all settings, but staff who work in some pre-schools have a particularly limited time, as their room may have to be vacated promptly at the end of each session. Staff in any setting may find that they have no option other than to write reports at home. This is not ideal, as confidentiality can become an issue. So, how can records be kept updated during the sessions, without staff feeling that they are neglecting the children? The answer is in the planning of the day/session. Staff should work co-operatively to ensure that all children are being well cared for, as each person takes time out to observe and record the development of the children in their group. The planning for this needs to be given a lot of thought.

For those settings that do not have a system in place, a staff meeting could be held to discuss the options for effective record keeping. Your support worker can give you advice about this.

What do you need to do?

If children feel secure, happy in their environment, respected and well cared for by the staff responsible for them, they will learn and develop. Children with anxieties about the care provided will be unsettled. Children become anxious

about things that are sometimes overlooked - a staff member, possibly a key worker leaving her job - 'Who will look after me now?' - or structural changes to the premises - 'The place will look different. I might get lost.'

If children are to feel secure, they should be kept informed in simple terms about what is going on. This obviously depends on their age, but children who overhear discussions about changes may be worried about what this will mean for them. Some children may not be able to express how they feel and say what is the cause of their anxiety. Look for facial expressions and any changes to their usual behaviour - this may be the indicator you need to determine that the child has a problem.

Relationships matter, whether you are thinking about your relationships with the parents, your relationships with the children, or the children's relationships with each other. You are the role model in your setting. How do you greet everyone each day? Do you offer praise for each child's efforts? Do you recognise the parents as the primary carers of their children? Developing positive relationships all round will enable children to feel confident about you and your setting, and encourage them to be more independent. Give children time to achieve. Many settings provide a wide range of activities for the children, and then rush the children through the activity in order to move on to the next one. Consider the children's personal development and give them:

■ **Time - to get ready to go outside.**
Allow time for the children to put their own coats/hats/boots on, and for taking them off. Fine motor skills will be developed just by doing up buttons, fastening shoe buckles and pulling up zips. Build this time into your outdoor play time.

- **Time - to go to the toilet.**
Allow children to go to the toilet whenever they need to, and not just an 'all together' rushed time before meals. Allow the children to spend time learning how to use the toilet appropriately, to wash their hands thoroughly, and make sure that the taps are switched off.

- **Time - to complete activities.** Allow the children as much time as they need to complete a task or finish making something. A real sense of satisfaction could be lost for the child who has to leave something unfinished. It may be that you have to stop, as lunchtime is approaching. Do you explain this to the child, and say 'That looks great. Let's put it on the side until after lunch, and then you can finish it ready to take home.' Or do you call out 'Tidy up time!' The child is left with an unfinished piece of construction or painting and no opportunity to finish it later.

- **Time - for the child.** How often do you just stop to listen to a child? Do you sit down with children and let them tell you in their own time about their news? Do you allow them the opportunity to express how they feel about, for example, a new baby in the family, the death of a pet, their holiday? Do you explain why their behaviour has not been acceptable, giving them a real understanding of right and wrong? Do you set a good example yourself, in the way you find time to talk to parents, other staff, visitors? All of these things will give out the right message for children - this person has time for me!

This standard covers care, learning and play. The word 'learning' in itself implies 'education'. Many carers think that children should not be offered formal learning at what appears to be a younger and younger age. Shouldn't children be able to learn naturally through play alone? Are worksheets the right way for young children to learn? There are so many views on this subject - how are you going to help the children in your care to develop to their potential?

The Qualifications and Curriculum Authority (QCA) says: 'The term 'curriculum' is used to describe everything that children do, see, hear and feel in their setting, both planned and unplanned.'

It is the word 'curriculum' that brings about so much discussion in childcare settings. However, if you think about this definition from the QCA, you will see that, no matter which play opportunities the children are engaged in, they will either be doing, seeing, hearing or feeling as part of the play. Here's a play activity:

Two children are building with the Lego bricks - no staff intervention.

They intend to build a tower, therefore they are **doing** - making something.

They have to use hand to eye co-ordination for this task, therefore they are **seeing** - focusing with their eyes to ensure that bricks are lined up correctly.

They are co-operating with each other to make sure that the tower is the height they want it to be, without falling over – problem-solving, therefore they are **hearing** one another.

They have completed their tower, and it stands alone. A real achievement - therefore they **feel** good!

This is a simple example, although there are many ways to describe doing, seeing, hearing and feeling, depending on the activity, such as:

- Doing a task, directed by an adult

- Hearing a story

- Seeing seeds grow

- Feeling in the sense of exploring textures - cornflour, for example.

Activities for all age groups should be planned around the curriculum, and they should be fun! Children will develop if they enjoy what they are doing, and if the staff are enjoying themselves, too. Children notice if staff are disinterested.

What activities do you plan for? Are they appropriate for the age of the children, and are all staff clear about the aims for the activities, in terms of the children's development?

Are staff who work with the three- to six-year-olds aware of the Foundation Stage curriculum, and working towards the Early Learning Goals? Your EYDCP support workers or early years teachers will be able to give advice about the curriculum.

Do all the staff know of all of the resources that are available to them in your setting, to ensure that children can make choices? Do they provide a wide range of play materials?

Don't forget the under twos in the planning process. There is an annex at the end of the standards document about care of the under twos, and the inspector will want to know, in connection with Standard 3, how you meet the needs of the youngest children.

In rooms accommodating no more than 12 babies/children under two years, staff should make sure that a range of sensory

play opportunities are available. Records should be kept on each child, as with the older children. Additional records on sleep, feeding and nappy changes will also be necessary.

The role of the adult is crucial. The inspector will expect to see plenty of interaction between the carers and children. How are relationships between the staff in your setting? Children pick up on differences and difficulties. Staff should work professionally together for the good of the children. Does your setting operate on two floors? Do staff have the opportunity to meet together, other than at arranged staff meetings? You may consider allowing children of different ages to spend time together during the day, and this will allow staff to work alongside colleagues they would not normally work with. This is good practice, and beneficial to the children.

Are older children involved in planning activities? Children enjoy being a part of what is going on - let your setting become more child led in respect of some activities. Let them decide what resources they need for the activity they have chosen - a good opportunity for

children to do some problem-solving.

When planning your topic and activities for the term, think about:

■ what the children will gain from this

■ how much adult intervention is needed

■ what skills the children will acquire

■ whether the topic is relevant to the time of year or related to a national event.

Make the topic interesting for the children. All efforts and abilities should be praised. If a child becomes confident, they will feel good about themselves. The advantage to children learning through play is that play can be spontaneous, just for the fun of it, and mistakes do not matter. Let children experiment - give them time - they will learn from their mistakes. Children will come to be aware of their own strengths and build on them. If they feel safe in the physical sense, they will explore further, in the knowledge that an adult is there if

needed. If they feel safe in the emotional sense, they will feel secure. Building children's self-esteem is very important. They can feel undermined if there is criticism, punishment or unfair comparisons to others. Always encourage children to do their best, and then praise whatever they do. Children should be given time to acquire skills.

Good practice
Consider:
■ Your information to parents - do they fully understand the way you approach the curriculum for their child?

■ How child centred is your setting - or is it very much staff directed? Find a balance.

■ Staff relationships - is there a real team feel to your setting? Is your staffing consistent, or are you losing staff regularly? Why?

■ Written information is necessary, but not a substitute for informing parents verbally about their child's development. How often do you hold parent's evenings? Can parents talk to you at any time about the care/education of their child?

What will the inspector be looking for?
Your plans and records - *written evidence*

How you use your observations and other information to help plan appropriate activities for the next steps in children's development and learning - *verbal discussion*

How you help three- and four-year-olds, for whom you receive funding, make progress towards the Early Learning Goals described in the *Curriculum Guidance for the Foundation Stage - written records and verbal discussion*

Dealing with dilemmas
You are caring for a group of children aged three to five years, and the day is coming to an end. A parent arrives to collect their child and asks them 'What have you been doing today?' The child replies 'Nothing!' The parent looks at you, and asks why the child has not made anything to bring home. How will you respond to this?

1. Explain that all the children have had a busy day, which does not necessarily mean that they have 'made' something to bring home.

2. The children have played games today, which meant they had to take turns, and perhaps learn how to lose a game (personal and social development).

3. The children have listened to a story, and talked about their own news (language and literacy).

4. The children have helped at snack time, with placing cups on tables, offering pieces of fruit to everyone, watching and talking to the staff about the fruit - halves, quarters, amounts - and then eaten it! (mathematical knowledge).

5. They played on the balancing beams in the garden this morning (physical development).

The message to the parent is - children do not have to produce something to prove that they have achieved.

The standard to be reached:
The registered person meets children's individual needs and promotes their welfare. They plan and provide activities and play opportunities to develop children's emotional, physical, social and intellectual capabilities.

Most registered childminders care for up to six children aged between nought and eight years at any one time. Consideration will need to be given to:

- Each child as an individual, with their own specific needs

- How you intend to provide activities for all ages of children in your care

- How involved the children are in planning activities

- How you relate to children, and how they relate to one another

- What resources you have available - can the children choose?

- Plans for indoor and outside play - how is this managed?

- The respect for each child's cultural and religious beliefs

- How you encourage children to experiment and try new things

A childminder has a wealth of everyday resources that can be used for the children to promote play, such as:

A blanket over a table - a great place to make a den!

Saucepans and wooden spoons

Newspapers/magazines/scissors/glue

Dough

Cardboard boxes

All of these things (and many others) will encourage children to use their imaginations - you don't need to spend a lot of money to give children play opportunities. A walk to the local shop to buy a pint of milk and post a letter will give you a good opportunity to help the children progress in all areas of development. Think about the money needed to buy the milk, the opportunity to discuss what happens to the letter that is to be posted, what you may see on the way to the shop, road safety, physical exercise, and more!

Many childminders make written records on the children in their care, especially those childminders who are part of a network. Parents appreciate the information shared with them about their child's day, as well as the noting of any significant developmental progress. Your support worker can advise you on systems for record keeping, and how you can share information with parents on their child's development.

You are offering a home from home setting, which is familiar to children. Routine is important - you may be organising the school run, fitting in a baby's feed, considering activities for the toddler in your care. Finding the right balance to meet all the children's needs, so that they are offered interesting activities to promote their all-round development, as well as time to relax, is not easy. The key to meeting this standard is in how you plan ahead for the next day/week.

The weather is always a factor, so if you had planned to be outside, and the weather lets you down, what other things can you do with children? Always have alternative play ideas ready.

Do you let the children choose from your range of play materials? Are your play resources easily seen and reached by the children? Do you encourage the children to suggest things to do, and then respond positively to their suggestions?

Talk to the children, be interested in their views, give them time to express themselves, value their comments, and encourage them in what they do. Your support worker can give you advice on how to provide a range of activities for all age groups.

Physical environment

The standard to be reached:
The premises are safe, secure and suitable for their purpose. They provide adequate space in an appropriate location, are welcoming to children and offer access to the necessary facilities for a range of activities which promote their development.

Requirement that you must comply with:
Children Act regulations
You must notify Ofsted if any changes are made to the premises or their use.

The premises, indoors and outside, need to be carefully thought about in terms of:

- The children's safety
- Cleaning and maintenance
- Temperature
- Space for the children to play, eat and rest
- Storage
- Toilets and nappy change areas
- Staff, kitchen and laundry facilities
- Arrangements for evacuation
- Pets

What does this mean for your setting?

Every setting is different. You may be working on school premises, in a village hall, a house converted for nursery use, or be in your own home as a registered childminder. Your setting may be on more than one floor, and the ages you are responsible for will vary from nought to eight years.

How can you achieve this standard in your setting? You need to consider criteria points 4.1 - 4.20.

Your main concern should be the safety and well-being of the children in your care. Your premises need careful consideration, depending on the ages of the children. Security must be uppermost in your mind.

Consider the following:

The entrance area
- Is your entrance area welcoming? Do

you have a staff noticeboard, with photos showing who everyone is, which room/area they work in, their qualifications?

- Do you have a parents' noticeboard giving parents information about the setting, the current topics and so on?

- Do you have a welcome poster written in different languages, so that all families, including those whose first language is not English, can feel welcome? How are parents and children verbally welcomed into the setting?

- Is the security of the building and outdoor play areas adequate?

The playrooms/outdoor areas
- Are the rooms warm and inviting?

- Are the staff involved with children's play?

- Are age appropriate play materials being offered to the children?

- Are all children able to access play materials?

- Are there displays, photos and examples of the children's work on the walls, at a height that the children can see?

- Is the outdoor area enclosed, with a locked gate?

- Are staff vigilant about unwanted visitors?

- Do you provide separate areas for quiet times, messy times and so on?

- Do you think about the groups of children in each room? Large or small groups? Some children work better in smaller groups.

- Are children under the age of two cared for in a large open-plan room? A smaller room is preferable – with a more homely feel. Allow the babies space to practice crawling and walking.

- Are your chairs and tables child sized?

- Do you provide comfortable adult chairs for staff feeding babies?

- Are your floor coverings suitable for their purpose, in other words, washable surface in the wet play area and carpeted area near books?

- Who is responsible for the regular cleaning and disinfecting of toys? The play areas should be clean and toys well maintained.

What do you need to do?

There is a lot to think about in respect of the premises. The registered person is not able to consider the physical environment on their own. It is everyone's responsibility to ensure the safety and well-being of the children in the setting. Parents should be asked always to close and lock the gate, and know not to allow other parents into the building when no member of staff is present. Staff need to make sure that the premises are clean, well ventilated, and should check the whole area - indoors and outside - before the day/session starts.

You must have a telephone on site. Some settings have a phone installed, others use mobile phones. You must be able to contact parents, as well as the emergency services. Do all the parents have the contact number for your setting? Do you keep a list of numbers for emergencies near to the phone?

The temperature in your setting will vary according to the time of day, time of year, and the changeable weather pattern in this country. A thermometer is used by many settings who try to keep the temperature to around 17 degrees centigrade. There is no hard and fast rule on this. Adequate heating and ventilation should be a part of a healthy environment. Diffusers over fluorescent strip lighting are advisable, for safety reasons, as well as to take away some of the direct strong light.

Space

Play space needs to be kept clear to allow the children to move freely. You should not include corridors or hallways in your calculations for play space.

The standard written in bold print does not state the space standard for each age group. However, the guidance book helps you with this, and is useful when working out approximately how many children could be accommodated in each area.

Age of child	Square metres
Under 2 years	3.5
2-3 years	2.5
3-8 years	2.3

How do you work this out?

1. Measure the total area of your playroom/play area.

2. Depending on the age of the children to be cared for in that room/area, divide the total area measurement by the square metres allowed for that age group.

3. You will have a number to give you an idea of how many children can be accommodated.

If you need help with your calculations, you can ask your support worker. The inspector will ask you how many children you hope to accommodate in each room. You can reply that you have based your calculations on the criteria set out under Standard 4 in your book. The inspector will not measure to confirm, unless they feel that you are trying to accommodate more children than would seem reasonable. It would be fair to say that most settings would request numbers of children to meet the staff ratios for the age group. For example, 24 children aged three to five in one room in a pre-school with three members of staff caring for them. This works out as one member of staff to every eight children.

How do you manage the space for children? Do you consider the noise levels in larger areas? Constant noise can disrupt children. Does your setting have individual rooms? This is preferable to open-plan areas, where people are constantly walking through to other areas. Think about the children. This is the area where they are being cared for - make it homely and inviting. Are the sleep rooms separate for the youngest children? Peace and quiet is necessary. Does your space allow for babies who are becoming mobile, and those who are not yet attempting to move? There is much to think about in respect of space - imagine yourself as the child, and what you would like.

Storage

When considering storage of play materials, think about the following:

- Is the storage area accessible to all staff, who store the materials safely?

- Do you have an inventory of all play materials, so that broken items can be replaced? You may consider making one person responsible for this in your setting.

- Larger items, such as pushchairs, need storage space, too. The larger items should not be left in areas where access from the building may be needed.

- Outside, the shed used for storage should be locked, and all outdoor play things should be carefully stacked, so that the risk of accidents relating to falling equipment is as small as possible.

- Storing cleaning materials in locked cupboards is necessary, too, for obvious safety reasons. The inspector will ask you where cleaning materials are kept. Are all staff aware of their responsibility to keep the cupboard locked at all times when the children are present? This could be included in your induction procedures.

Toilets

Although the allowance for toilets for children in your setting is not written in the bold print, most settings do work within the criteria under 4.12: 'There is a minimum of one toilet and one handwash basin with hot and cold water available for every ten children over the age of two years'. Other points to bear in mind include:

- The hot water should be thermostatically controlled so that no child can be burned.

- Towels and flannels are used in some settings, paper towels in others. Hot air dryers may be too hot, and should be tested by staff first.

- Nappy changing facilities should be provided where necessary, with consideration given to children who are being toilet trained, too. The nappy change areas are important. For hygiene purposes, staff should wear protective plastic aprons and latex gloves when changing nappies.

- Where the toilets are situated is important. If children are to become independent, they should be able to access the toilet area at the appropriate age. If they have to walk some distance, or leave their play area, a member of staff will need to accompany them - this could affect your ratios.

Facilities

- **Staff room:** not all settings have a staff room. For example, a pre-school or after-school club is unlikely to have one, as the time spent with the children is four hours or less. A day nursery, however, where staff are usually on site from 8am-6pm should have a room or quiet area for staff on their breaks. Some nursery owners insist that the staff remain on site even if they are not working, as everyone would be needed if the building had to be evacuated. In this case, the staff should have somewhere to go, away from the children, to enjoy their well-deserved break time.

- **Kitchen:** many settings have a kitchen, and the general rule is that children have no access to the kitchen. A gate is placed across the doorway so that no child can enter the room. In those settings where children may have access, the following points should be considered:

Children must always be supervised in kitchen areas.

Your risk assessment of the room - hot cooker, access to knives and so on.

For those settings that have the use of the kitchen for preparing main meals for children, the local environmental health department will advise on what needs to be considered in respect of handwash basins, correct storage of food, and the cook should have completed a food handling course.

- **Laundry:** safety and hygiene rules would not allow for children to enter a laundry room in a nursery. However, in some settings, a washing machine may have been installed in the area where nappies are changed. In this situation, a risk assessment by staff should lead them to agree that no child should be left unsupervised in the area.

- Electrical items should always be out of reach of children, and annual testing of portable appliances, such as kettles and microwaves, should be carried out by a qualified electrician.

Evacuation

Evacuation of the premises should be practised termly. In this way, the registered person will be sure that children can always be removed from the building safely and quickly. The premises should always be evacuated promptly. Are you sure that the routes for evacuation are always clear? There should never be any equipment blocking the exits. How do you make sure that everyone is evacuated? Apart from the children and staff, remember visitors, students and parents.

Pets

If you keep pets, their health and well-being is important if you want to keep the children well and not open to infection. Care of the pets should not be overlooked. Children like to help and this is not a problem as long as you follow strict hygiene rules.

Good practice

- Quality of care will be affected if the premises are not well planned. Think about the layout of your building to make sure that there is a welcoming feel, inviting play areas, pride in staff appearance, and recognition of the children's achievements.

- Consistency of staff makes a big difference - people who know the building well, what resources are available, and have good working relationships with one another.

- Within the planning, staff recognise the need for each child to have some time on a one-to-one basis, and that, if a parent wishes to discuss their child, a quiet area can be found for the discussion. Make the premises family friendly.

What will the inspector be looking for?

Your access to a telephone - *visual evidence*

How you meet space requirements and organise space - *visual and written evidence and discussion*

Toilet facilities and arrangements for nappy changing - *visual evidence and discussion*

Where you keep confidential information - *visual evidence*

Staff facilities - *verbal discussion*

Facilities where staff and parents can speak confidentially - *verbal discussion*

Kitchen and laundry facilities - *visual evidence and verbal discussion*

Planning permission - *if this applies at your inspection*

Anyone else using the premises or other parts of the building - *verbal discussion*

Your procedures if you use public playgrounds - *written evidence*

Dealing with dilemmas

You manage a day nursery where 50 children aged nought to five years are accommodated. The mornings are always busy, as many parents arrive at the same time to drop off their children. Normally, a member of staff is in the area to allow the parents in.

However, on this occasion, the member of staff has answered the phone, leaving the main entrance for a couple minutes. The door bell rings, and as a parent leaves the building, they allow the person who rang the bell to enter without the member of staff being aware. The person enters the toddler playroom and is not recognised by staff in the room.

The person is approached, and asked 'Can I help you?' The person, a male, replies 'I was just hoping to see my son today. His name is John. Can I see him please?' The staff in the room are aware that John's parents have recently divorced, and that there is a court order stating that John's father should have no access to him. John is not on the premises. What should happen now?

1. It is right that the staff should be aware of the court order, and right that they should approach anyone who is not known to them. John's father must not be left alone at any time.

2. One member of staff should go immediately to fetch the person in charge, manager or deputy. The staff member with John's father should explain that the manager or deputy will be able to help. All staff must remain calm.

3. The manager/deputy should invite John's father to the office to talk about his visit. He will need to made aware that a copy of the court order is on the premises, and that the staff would be unable to allow access to John when he arrives for his nursery session.

   This could be difficult, and so a member of staff should be in attendance also. John's father must be asked gently to leave, and contact his solicitor for help. He must be seen to leave the premises.

4. John's father would not have gained access if the member of staff had not left her post, but this could happen - the phone could ring at any time.

5. Parents must be reminded never to let each other in unless a member of staff is in the area.

6. If you are on door duty, make sure that you stay there - if you have to do something, call on someone else to cover you.

Standard 4
Childminding

The standard to be reached:
The premises are safe, secure and suitable for their purpose.
They provide adequate space in an appropriate location, are welcoming to children and have access to the necessary facilities for a range of activities which promote their development.

As a registered childminder, your premises are individual to you. Registrations have been approved in town houses (more than two storeys), flats, bungalows as well as two storey houses. How will you ensure that your physical environment can meet the standard? You need to consider criteria points 4.1 - 4.11.

The inspector will need to know that you have planning permission, so all documents relating to this will need to be provided. Space allowance for all the ages of children will be discussed with you.

You know your home best. Think about where the children will be able to play, eat and rest. Is your home cluttered, or have you given thought to how much room you give the children?

■ Is your garden suitable for play? The inspector will ask to see the outdoor play area. Your registration course will have helped you to consider your garden in respect of safety - gates, plants, greenhouse, pond. What play equipment do you have, and is it well maintained?

■ Do you care for children overnight? You will need to be able to show the inspector where children will sleep, and discuss what arrangements you have made with the parents about overnight care.

■ How welcoming is your home? Is there evidence of children's work anywhere? Do you allow time when the children arrive in the morning to speak to the parents, and welcome them into your home - even if they are in a hurry? Think about the positive message that the child will receive if you invite their parents in for a chat at either end of the day.

■ Do the children have access to your kitchen? Consider all the safety aspects that you discussed on your registration course. Have you made the kitchen safe?

■ How do you meet the varying needs of the children in your care? Think about your premises. Do you allow the children to play unsupervised anywhere in the home, for example if they are older. Do the children use the toilet independently? Can they lock themselves in? All of these things need consideration in a childminder's home.

Equipment

The standard to be reached:
Furniture, equipment and toys are provided which are appropriate for their purpose and help to create an accessible and stimulating environment. They are of suitable design and condition, well maintained and conform to safety standards.

Whatever type of setting you work in, equipment will be needed. You should have a list of necessary equipment for each area/room, and work to that list, ensuring that you are providing for all age groups. You will need to consider all the equipment in your setting to be certain that you will reach the required standard. You need to consider criteria points 5.1 - 5.3.

What does this mean for your setting?
Meeting the needs of all the children who attend your setting is important, and

the equipment you provide must be safe. This standard looks closely at the following:

■ Toys and play equipment

■ Furniture

■ Safety issues

The toys and play equipment you provide for all ages must conform to British Standards (BS). The kite mark is an obvious sign of a good standard - you may be aware of this on the windows in your setting. There is also a European Standard (EN) mark on equipment. If in doubt, always check with the manufacturers about the equipment you are considering purchasing. When choosing toys for your setting, look for the lion mark (a triangle with a lion face) which means that the toys have been made to a high standard for this country and Europe.

Allow for enough toys for the children to share and play with. Present them well - keep them clean and well maintained. Children's development should be considered when toys/play equipment are provided. Do you think about reflecting our multicultural society when you are choosing play materials? For example, do you have a wok in the play house, dressing-up clothes that reflect other cultures, books and jigsaws that show positive images of men and women and differing abilities?

The environment should be stimulating and interesting for all age groups. Do you provide a range of materials so that the children can experiment in art and craft activities? Do you include music in your early years curriculum, with opportunities for children to learn rhythm and beat? Do you provide activities for all age groups to encourage the use of the senses - sight, hearing, touch, taste and smell?

Toys break and will need replacing from time to time. You need to have a clear policy on replacing toys and play equipment that will need reviewing regularly. An inventory of all play equipment is the best way to keep track of what is available for all the children. A leaflet on toy safety is available from the National Toy Council, 80 Camberwell Road, London SE5 OEG Tel: 020 7701 7271.

Furniture is necessary in every setting. From tables and chairs to cupboards, the registered person needs to be satisfied that the furniture is sturdy, and not likely to be broken easily. Fittings such as stair gates should be available where necessary. In some settings, for example, they are used to prevent children from entering the kitchen. The gates should conform to BS number 4125. If you have any questions about the safety of equipment in your setting, you can ask advice from your support worker, or call the Royal Society for the Prevention of Accidents (ROSPA) on 0121 248 2000.

Safety issues must be uppermost in your mind when caring for young children, who may not recognise danger. It is the responsibility of the registered person to make sure that all toys, play equipment and furniture is safe. You may think about designating the job of checking toys for safety to one person, who takes the responsibility of keeping the inventory updated, too.

What do you need to do?

Think about all the equipment in your setting, not just the toys and play equipment.

■ Do you have a smoke alarm that operates by battery? Check the batteries at least once a year.

■ Buggies, pushchairs and prams need maintaining - when did you last check these?

■ Electrical equipment, such as a television, kettle, plug-in radio, are all subject to safety checks as part of your responsibility.

■ All portable heaters should be BS approved, and checked annually by a qualified person.

Regular inspection of equipment in your setting is necessary if you are to provide a safe environment for the children. You need to check the condition of all play equipment at the start and end of each day/session.

Dealing with dilemmas

You work in the baby room of your setting. Today, only six babies aged nine months to two years are present. You are sitting on the floor, playing with some of the children, when you hear a cry. One baby, moving around the room in a baby walker, has slid through the side of the walker, and toppled onto another child sitting nearby. Both children are crying, and the baby walker is in a state of collapse. What do you do?

1. The priority must be to comfort both children, as one person removes the baby walker from the room. The children must be checked for injury, and this must be recorded if either child is hurt.

2. Once the children are settled again, the baby walker must be checked, to establish what has caused the problem. In this situation, the wing nuts have come loose, and the material holding the baby up has slipped off the frame. The material is rather worn. This means that the material could have frayed at any time, causing a baby to collapse to the floor.

3. The material will need replacing, and the wing nuts secured tightly, but what about the future? Staff must now regularly check the baby equipment - the high chairs, cots, buggies, baby walkers. How often do your staff check the equipment in the baby room? Do high chairs get checked, or are they just wiped over after each meal? Are cots checked for loose fittings? Remember, if a child should fall from a cot where the side was not fully up, the child could suffer a nasty accident. Always check and then double check the sides on a cot before leaving a baby/young child to sleep. Do the buggies and pushchairs have regular maintenance to ensure that they are safe at all times?

4. Who needs to be told about this? The manager or supervisor should be informed immediately. If either of the children were hurt, an accident report must be filled in, and the parents made aware, and their signature sought. In this situation, neither child was hurt.

The manager needs to think carefully about risk assessment of all equipment in the setting. When was the last time everything was thoroughly checked? Now is the time to put a procedure into place to make sure that staff check equipment before children use anything.

You may, as part of your routine, take the children off the premises to play in the local park, where swings and slides are available. Although you are not directly responsible for the safety of the park equipment, you should still ensure that the equipment is safe for the children in your care. If you notice that something is broken, keep the children away from the area, and report the matter to your local council/person responsible, when you return to your setting.

Is second hand, second best? This is a question that is often asked in day care settings. Should everything be new? If you wish to be as sure as you can be that your equipment is safe - buy new. You will have a manufacturers' guarantee - you will not get this from a second-hand purchase. If you do decide to buy or loan second-hand goods, be clear about where the item has come from. After all, it may be that the buggy, for example, is not second hand - but third or even fourth hand. If you know the history of the piece of equipment, you may decide to take the risk - but it will be a risk all the same.

Good practice

■ Young children do not recognise danger in the way adults do. They do not see the need for checking things before playing with them. The toy is there - 'I want it now'. Adults should check equipment before the session starts, as the equipment is being put out.

■ All play equipment should conform, where applicable, to the highest standards of quality. Anything checked by a qualified person will result in a certificate of satisfactory standard - display these certificates. Parents will be reassured to note that you have the equipment checked regularly.

What will the inspector be looking for?

How you make sure that your furniture, toys and equipment are safe - *verbal discussion*.

The inspector will ask what measures you take to ensure that all equipment is in good enough order for use. The inspector will consider if:

■ the toys, furniture and equipment meet the needs of all the children in your setting;

■ the items are in a safe condition;

■ the equipment is easily accessed by the children;

■ you have considered including everyone - equal opportunity in play.

The standard to be reached:
Furniture, equipment and toys are provided which are appropriate for their purpose and help to create an accessible and stimulating environment. They are of suitable design and condition, well maintained and conform to safety standards.

Unlike in a group setting, the childminder has a home environment to consider, with all the equipment that is usually found in a domestic property. You need to consider criteria points 5.1 - 5.4.

The inspector will talk to you about your home, what toys and play materials you offer, and whether you offer a sufficient range of toys for all age groups in your care. You will be able to show the inspector where your toys and play equipment are kept, and discuss the range you have available. Children should be able to access the toys - allowing for choice.

The inspector will ask you about your understanding of providing children of different ages with suitably sized furniture, and age appropriate equipment. You will be able to indicate to the inspector what equipment you have available for all of the children, and which is suitable for the different ages.

The inspector will ask you about what safety measures you have in

place for toys, furniture and equipment. You should be able to talk about your understanding of buying quality items that will last, and are sturdy. Ideally, equipment is purchased from new. You also check all equipment regularly for breakages/wear and tear.

You may be asked about what play materials you offer the children. On your registration course, you will have discussed what play opportunities you could offer children in your home. You will have considered the use of natural play materials, as well as bought toys. You may have considered household items for the children to play with, such as junk modelling, making a shop from your grocery cupboard. Use your home setting to its full advantage.

The inspector may ask about maintenance of the equipment you use indoors and outside. You should be able to explain how you check the equipment before and after use to ensure that all equipment remains in good condition. This would include pushchairs, cots, highchairs, car seats, large garden play equipment, as well as smaller items used for play.

Are you aware of the British Standards (BS), European Standards (EN) and lion marks? They are a sign of quality toy and equipment items. You should look for these when you buy new equipment.

The main emphasis for Standard 5 is that you make sure that the furniture, toys and equipment are safe for the children in your care.

Safety

The standard to be reached:
The registered person takes positive steps to promote safety within the setting and on outings and ensures proper precautions are taken to prevent accidents.

Requirement that you must comply with: Children Act regulations
You must keep a statement of the procedures to be followed in the event of a fire.

- The Health and Safety at Work Act 1974
- The Health and Safety (Information for Employees) Regulations 1989
- Health and Safety (First Aid) Regulations 1981
- The Control of Substances Hazardous to Health Regulations 1988
- The Reporting of Injuries, Diseases and Dangerous Occurrences Regulations 1985 (RIDDOR)
- The Electricity at Work Regulations 1989
- Food Hygiene Regulations 1995
- Food Safety (temperature control) Regulations 1995

Although the registered person/people are responsible for the safety of everyone in the setting, this cannot be considered by them alone. The manager/ supervisor, staff, visitors, parents and older children - in other words, anyone who is on the premises at any time - have a responsibility regarding safety issues.

What does this mean for your setting?

Safety, indoors and outside, needs to be considered. The following points are relevant to all settings:
- Health and safety regulations
- Risk assessment
- Gas and electricity
- Security
- Supervision
- Outside areas
- Water
- Hazardous plants
- Fire safety
- Outings and transport
- Insurance

You need to consider criteria points 6.1 - 6.13.

What do you need to do?
Health and safety regulations

A health and safety policy and procedures is your starting point. All documents relating to policies and procedures are considered in more detail under Standard 14 in this book. However, you need to think about the specific safety issues under this standard. Your policies and procedures will state how you intend to ensure the safety of everyone connected to the setting. There is legislation that you must be aware of. At times, the legislation changes, and so you need to keep up to date with the changes as they affect you. The main legislation is the Children Act 1989, and the Care Standards Act 2000. These state your responsibilities in caring for young children. You will not be expected to recite the Children Act or let the inspector know about your understanding of the Care Standards Act.

The books you have been given that you are working with - the National Standards and guidance books - give you the relevant information you need to comply with the requirements of the Children Act.

It is likely that your local EYDCP team/ support workers will provide training for you to ensure that you and the staff have an understanding of the health and safety requirements. This training will cover such issues as induction for new staff who are unaware of your policies and procedures, delegating specific safety tasks to staff, putting together a safety booklet for your setting, how to carry out risk assessments, and how parents and children can be made aware of safety issues in the setting.

The legislation that you will need to be aware of is:

You are not alone in finding out about the legislation. Other than contacting your local support worker, you will find a useful appendix at the end of your guidance book – 'Organisations and publications which can provide useful sources of information'.

Your parents' information leaflet should state that the welfare and safety of the children is of paramount importance in your setting. Parents should be made aware that they have a part to play in this. Safety issues could be discussed at parents' evenings, when you can reinforce the issues that parents seem to forget. The best example of this is closing the gate when you leave. It always surprises staff that parents want to know how you will keep their children safe, and then leave the gate open as they leave! A clearly worded notice on the gate acts as a reminder. However, some parents need to be verbally reminded as well.

Risk assessment

What does this term mean? All staff working in your setting should be aware of their responsibility to make sure the premises are safe at all times, and a risk assessment is the way to achieve this.

Daily - the premises should be looked at by staff caring for the children, in terms of a safety check before anything is used. It may be that you work in a setting that is multi-use, and in the evenings other users have had access to your pre-school room, after-school club room or nursery.

As equipment is set up, safety checks should be made to ensure that accidents are unlikely to happen through, for example, loose fittings. The outdoor areas are equally important. Bottles may have been thrown over the fence into the play area, and it is not unheard of for needles from drug users to be found. Staff must be vigilant at all times to these types of hazards.

Regularly - all equipment must be maintained. Are high chairs and cots checked by staff? Is all play equipment in good working order?

How do you record your risk assessments? You could provide a book that is kept in one place for everyone to use. A simple form for people to fill in could include the following details: date; time; what was checked; by whom; action needed; reported; action taken, by whom, and on what date.

In this way, all staff can make sure that their own task in checking an area of the setting has been seen to be done, and recorded. If action needs to be taken, for example, there is a broken piece of equipment, the member of staff should also report the matter verbally to the senior member of staff, after they have removed the broken item.

Be clear - it is the responsibility of the registered person to ensure everyone's safety. It is the responsibility of people working and using the setting to report any safety issue for the registered person to address. If a written format is used, as well as verbally informing a senior person of the problem, action can be taken quickly.

The stages of any risk assessment are:

1. Recognition - identifying the hazards that are present.

2. Evaluation - decide who might be harmed.

3. The risks - evaluating the extent of the risks involved.

4. Control - introducing the measures to combat/reduce the identified risks.

5. Record any significant findings.

6. Monitor and review the situation.

Gas and electricity

No-one in your setting would be expected to check the services you use, in respect of gas and electricity - this would not be a part of your risk assessment. You are responsible, however, for making sure that all appliances are safe. This can be done through a qualified person, working with gas and/or electricity. The appliances you use can be checked annually. Certificates stating that the check has been carried out are usually produced. With electrical items, such as kettles and microwave cookers, small labels are sometimes stuck on the item as a record that they have been passed as satisfactory. This is known as PAT (portable appliance testing) and many settings have this arrangement in place with a qualified electrician. If you are an owner of a setting, this would be your responsibility. If you work on school premises, it is likely that the school has an arrangement for the whole site to be checked - but do make sure of this. Committees of pre-school settings and creche managers should also make sure that PAT is carried out, as the group may operate in multi-use buildings. The responsibility for any building is down to the owner or committee overseeing the building. If, for example, you work in a church or community hall, the hall committee has overall responsibility for the safety of the premises. Pre-school committees should work with the hall committee to advise them of safety issues that affect the day-to-day running of the setting.

Security

Depending on the ages of the children, keeping children on the premises can be difficult. During the holidays,

The Association of British Insurers
51 Gresham Street
London EC2V 7HQ
Tel: 0207 600 3333
Website: www.abi.org.uk

British Standards Institute (BSI)
Maylands Avenue
Hemel Hempstead HP2 4SQ
Tel: 01442 230442
Website: www.bsi-global.com

Chartered Institute of Environmental Health (CIEH)
Chadwick Court
15 Hatfields
London SE1 8DJ
Tel: 0207 928 6006
Website: www.cieh.org.uk
Publication - *Health and Safety - First Principles*

Department for Education and Skills (DfES)
DfES Publications
PO Box 5050
Sherwood Park
Annesley
Nottingham NG15 0DJ
Tel: 0845 602 2260
Website: www.dfes.gov.uk
Publications on a number of issues

Department for the Environment, Transport and the Regions (DETR)
Roads, Vehicles and Road Safety Division
Great Minster House
76 Marsham Street
London SWIP 4DR
Tel: 0207 944 8300
Website: www.roads.detr.gov.uk

Health and Safety Executive
HSE Books
PO Box 1999
Sudbury
Suffolk CO10 2WA
Tel: 01787 881 165
Website: www.hse.gov.uk

Publications:
Essentials for Health and Safety at Work

Five Steps to Risk Assessment

Everyone's Guide to RIDDOR

Brief Guide to the Control of Substances Hazardous to Health (COSHH) Regulations 1999

playschemes operate on some large school sites, and security is hard to manage. The inspector will want to know what system you have in place for ensuring that the children remain on site, and how you prevent unwanted visitors from entering. Staff working on playschemes can find the security a main issue - how can this be looked at for the playschemes as well as for other settings?

1. Know the site well, wherever you are working.

2. Know where the exits are, which areas of the building are not to be accessed. Are the doors locked, to prevent children moving into other areas?

3. Are older children aware of stranger danger?

4. Who is responsible for approaching unexpected visitors?

5. Do you all wear name badges, identifying yourselves as staff?

6. Are you all aware of the ways out of the building?

7. If there was a security risk, what would you do? Talk about this situation, as you may need to deal with it at some stage.

8. Where are the toilets? Do children have to walk some distance to reach the nearest toilets? How do you manage this on a large site?

Written policies and procedures are helpful, but all staff should communicate as well, to consider ways in which security can be effective for your setting.

Supervision

Children need to become independent, but depending on their age and developmental stage, they need to be supervised to ensure they come to no harm. Once you are satisfied that your risk assessment of the play areas has been carried out, the children should be encouraged to explore the environment. Think about the activity the children are engaged in - are they able to do this under constant supervision, or with you at a distance? The level of supervision depends on the children's ages and stages of development.

Outside areas
Think about the risks in the outdoor area:

■ Are the premises fenced in, with no footholds for the children to climb?

■ Is the gate secure?

■ Does the public have any access to the premises whilst the children play outside?

■ Are all of your large play equipment items in good condition, pegged down when necessary?

■ Is the surface on which the children play safe? Do you use bark as a base? Check for animal excrement before the children use the area.

■ Has your sandpit got a cover?

■ If children are able to go indoors and outside by choice, how are they supervised as they enter and leave the building?

■ Do you have adequate staffing in the garden?

■ Are the children dressed appropriately for the weather? Think about children near water - upturned containers that have collected rain. Think about snow and ice - children slipping over. Think about the plants in your garden - are they suitable for a children's play area?

Water
Never underestimate the dangers of water. Children do not always see the risks as you do - they will not understand until they are older that drowning can occur in a few inches of water. The areas of danger that the staff must recognise include:
Buckets and bowls
Goldfish tanks
Puddles
Water butts
Ponds
Hoses
Paddling pools
Bird baths

In other words, anywhere that water can be found.

Written parental permission should be obtained before taking children to water-based activities, such as the swimming pool or the sea. Allow children to play with water under staff supervision. This will form a part of your risk assessment. Always check the temperature of water that children have access to in their play. Empty the water tray when it is finished with. Mop up wet floors immediately, and allow to dry before allowing children into the area.

Remember: children should always be strictly supervised when they are playing with or near water.

Hazardous plants
In the back of your guidance book, there is an appendix relating to plants. The list is not comprehensive, and unless you would recognise the plants from the written name, this is not too helpful. There are good books available, such as *Poisonous Plants and Fungi - an Illustrated Guide* (The Stationery Office ISBN 0 11 242718 9) which not only describe the plants well, but have photos too, so that you can easily identify what you have growing in your garden that could be unsafe for the children. You can also visit your local garden centre to ask for advice on suitable plants for a children's garden.

Fire safety
To quickly and effectively remove the children to a place of safety in the case of a fire should be practised regularly, and without causing alarm to the children. Time your evacuations to satisfy yourself that the building was cleared quickly. You must have clear fire procedures in place, so that everyone is fully aware of their responsibilities. The fire officer will have visited your premises, and advised you on

a number of safety issues, for example, where to put fire extinguishers and smoke alarms.

The most important thing is to get everyone out of the building - leave the fire to the fire-fighters. Staff may have had training in the use of your fire equipment, but it is more important for the staff to evacuate the building than try to deal with the fire - buildings can be replaced, people can't. Your fire extinguishers should be checked annually.

Smoke alarms save lives - all settings should have at least one installed. The alarm should conform to British Standards.

Are your exits kept clear at all times to allow for a quick evacuation? You should practice leaving the building from different exits, as a fire may start near to the main exit you would use.

Outings and transport
Thought and preparation needs to be given to outings to ensure that they are a success. What do you need to think about?

- Where you are going – is it suitable for the ages of children in your care?

- Timings - depart and return

- The ages of the children - individual needs

- Ratios - are parents coming with you?

- Written parental permission

- Suitable transport - cars, coach, seatbelts

- Mobile phone

- First aid kit, and any medication required

- List of children and staff on outing - emergency contact details

- Risk assessment of the place you are going - a pre-visit by a member of staff, if possible.

Dealing with dilemmas

You have planned an outing to the library for eight of your three- to five-year-olds. The library is a short walking distance away from your setting. Two members of staff will be taking the children to the library, and this has been done many times before. Today, as the group make their way to the library, one member of staff stumbles on the pavement, twisting her ankle. What can the other member of staff do? Eight children need to be kept safe.

1. Ensure that the children stand well back from the road, and all stay side by side.

2. Check that the member of staff with the twisted ankle is as comfortable as possible.

3. Using the mobile phone, call the setting to ask for help. Explain clearly what has happened - the member of staff may need medical attention.

4. Stay with the children, keeping them occupied until help arrives.

Issues to consider before the outing:

Is the mobile phone fully charged?
Do you know the number for the setting?

Insurance

You must have insurance for the children in your care, and parents should be made aware that the insurance is in place. Do not display your actual certificate, which will state the amount of insurance you are covered for. A notice, giving the name of the insurance company, your policy number, and the year for which insurance is provided is all you need to display. A substantial level of cover is needed for your setting, and there are a number of insurance companies who specialise in insuring childcare settings. If you work in a building that is multi-use, this will need additional consideration, as you will not be the only group using the facilities - the insurers will advise you on this.

Good practice

■ Always look for potential danger – you cannot be too vigilant.

■ Make risk assessment a part of your everyday routine.

■ Encourage older children to be safety minded, without causing anxiety.

■ Name the staff responsible for safety in each area - delegate responsibility.

■ Include parents in the way in which safety is considered.

■ Your noticeboard could have a 'safety for all' section - issues for your setting

The guidance book suggests that you 'take a child's eye view of the premises, both inside and out, seeing the danger from their point of view'. This is good practice, and should be encouraged for all staff in your setting.

What will the inspector be looking for?

That you have complied with all health, fire and safety requirements/ recommendations - *visual and written evidence*

Your risk assessments - *verbal discussion, and written records*

Policies and procedures relating to safety - *written evidence*

Fire log book - *written evidence*

Public liability insurance - *notice on board, original certificate in office*

The standard to be reached:

The registered person takes positive steps to promote safety within the setting and on outings and ensures proper precautions are taken to prevent accidents.

There are a number of points to consider for safety in a childminder's home. You need to consider criteria points 6.1 - 6.18.

Reducing hazards: How do you do this?

You will have thought about all possible hazards in your home, and lessened the risk of accidents by moving unsafe items or equipment, and checking your resources regularly. Do you have your gas and electric appliances checked annually or serviced by a qualified engineer? Are you clear about your evacuation plan in case of a fire? Are you in agreement with the parents about outings, and your arrangements for the children's safety when you are off your premises?

Security: How conscious are you of the security of your home?

You will need to make sure that all older members of your family are clear about closing and locking doors, and being careful about who enters the property. Do you have window locks which allow the premises to be well-ventilated, but which prevent children opening windows too far?

Supervision: Are you with the children all the time?

This is not always possible - you may have a baby sleeping upstairs, a toddler in your sitting room with you, and two older children in the dining area, sitting at the table with jigsaws. As long as you are satisfied that the area in which the children are playing or resting is safe, and you check the children regularly, you will be supervising them.

Outside area: Is your garden safe?

The garden should be secure, with a locked gate. Children should always be supervised in the garden. Do you regularly check your outdoor play equipment? Are your sheds or garages where tools, garden equipment and decorating items are stored, locked? Do you check your garden for hazards before the children go out? Do you make sure that children cannot get in the greenhouse - they are a real hazard.

Water: Safe water play means good fun!

Enjoy the time you spend in the garden with the children - let them use the paddling pool, splash in puddles. Watch them at all times - if you have to go indoors, take the children with you -

never leave children with water unsupervised. Cover your pond with firm mesh that will take the weight of an adult, or fence the area off.

Hazardous plants: How well do you know your garden, and what is growing in it?

Books that explain the plants to avoid are available from booksellers or libraries. Your garden centre will also have information.

Kitchen: Potential dangers are all around

Many childminders do not allow access to the kitchen for minded children. If they do, strict supervision is needed. You will have discussed the dangers on your registration course, and be fully aware of the importance of cupboard locks and so on.

Insurance

Do you have current public liability insurance? The certificate should be made available for parents and the childcare inspector to see.

Health

The standard to be reached:
The registered person promotes the good health of children and takes positive steps to prevent the spread of infection and appropriate measures when they are ill.

Requirements that you must comply with:
Children Act regulations
You must keep a record of all medicines administered to children.

You must keep a signed record of all accidents to children, and notify Ofsted of any serious injury or death to any child in your care or adults on the premises.

You must notify Ofsted of any infectious disease that a qualified medical person considers notifiable.

What does this mean for your setting?

Promoting good health within your setting is to the benefit of all, and you should reflect this in your policies and procedures. You should do all you can to stem the spread of infection. Ofsted will need to be kept informed of any significant health matter, as described under the Children Act regulations. You need to consider criteria points 7.1 - 7.12 for this standard.

When thinking about the health of the children in your setting, the criteria points listed in your guidance books are:
- Hygiene
- Animals
- Sandpits
- Food handling
- Medicine
- First aid
- Sick children
- Smoking

What do you need to do?
Hygiene

Staff should maintain good hygiene practices within the setting. Personal hygiene for staff as well as children needs consideration:

- Hand washing after using the toilet, and before handling any food.

- Encourage children to blow their noses, and dispose of the tissue in a lidded bin.

- All staff should be aware of procedures to deal with bodily fluids, and their disposal.

A rota system will ensure that all necessary cleaning and checking is carried out. Whilst it is important for the setting to be kept clean, the actual cleaning should not interfere with the time that the children are being cared for. Consider the following:

- Do you have notices around your setting to remind adults to wash their hands?

- Do you keep nailbrushes and clean towels near to the washbasins?

- Are staff familiar with your health and safety policies and procedures? More importantly, do they follow the procedures in place? It is the responsibility of the registered person to ensure that the staff are aware of all procedures, and adhere to them. A poster showing common illnesses can be placed on the noticeboard, with any other health/hygiene information.

The environmental health officers will expect a good standard of hygiene in your setting. They can be contacted if you have any queries about environmental health issues.

Animals

Any pets on site should have their own care arrangements, with designated staff responsible for them. Children may like to help care for the pets, and be able to hold them. However, strict hygiene rules should be followed. Pet areas should be kept clean, and pet food should be stored in a closed container, not near other food. Pets, if out of their home, should be supervised.

Sandpits

Regular inspection of sandpits is necessary and this happens in most settings. What happens less frequently is the changing of the sand. This should not be overlooked. You can clean the sand, by sieving it.

Food handling

The person responsible for preparing and cooking the meals for the children should have a food handling certificate. This training can be arranged through your environmental health office. High standards of hygiene should be in place in the kitchen, and the cook should be clear about the procedures for maintaining the standards. Consider the following:

- Is open food kept covered?

- Is food ever prepared by someone who is unwell - suffering from an upset stomach? This should never happen.

Now wash your hands

- Do you have plants in the kitchen? They attract dust.

- Do you offer a balanced nutritional diet to all the children, taking allergies and cultural preferences into account? This should be discussed with the parents.

Medicine

Administering medicine to children needs to be properly organised. Who should be responsible for this? A room senior, deputy or manager should be responsible overall for all medications - never allow an unqualified person or student to give medication to a child.

Dosages, and the child's details, must be recorded, with a parent's signature written on the day, agreeing to you giving the child the prescribed medication. Consider the following:

- When liquid medicine is given to a child, does the member of staff pour from the opposite side of the bottle to the instructions? If any liquid spills down the side of the bottle, the wording on the instructions will not be smeared.

- Does the member of staff check the medicine has not passed the 'use by' date?

- What procedures are in place for children to be given their medication on outings?

- Are parents in agreement that you will only give prescribed medication? The only time you may administer another medication is for a teething baby. Parents sometimes ask carers to give their baby Calpol, or similar, for 'when you need it'. You must not give Calpol to a baby or young child in your care without the parent giving you written agreement first. Your medication consent form should be worded to allow for this. Usually, if a baby is unwell, and you are concerned about the teething, you may have to contact the parents - the baby may have a high temperature, and need to be taken home. Think about the baby's needs first.

First aid

There should always be a first aider on site. Parents should be informed of this. Staff who are trained in first aid should have a current certificate. The training has to be renewed every three years, so a rolling programme of training should be organised for your staff. A first aid box should be available on each floor of your setting, and someone should be responsible for keeping the boxes full. A typical first aid box should contain the following, as a minimum:

Individually wrapped sterile adhesive dressings (assorted) - plasters

Sterile eye pads

Triangular bandages individually wrapped - sterile if possible

Safety pins

Sterile wound dressings - medium and large sized

Disposable gloves

Individually wrapped alcohol free moist wipes

You can buy ready-made first aid kits in larger chemists. However, many settings use a large plastic container and buy the items they need separately.

Parental permission is needed for children to receive emergency treatment, and you should have a clear policy on how you advise parents of your emergency arrangements.

Accident records must be kept on site, in one place, so all staff can find them. For confidential reasons, parents should not be able to see records of other accidents when they sign for their child's accident. Your guidance book offers helpful advice on what information is needed for your accident record book:

Details of any existing injuries when a child arrives

The time, date and nature of any accident

Details (names) of the child(ren) affected

The type and location of any injury

The action taken, any subsequent action and by whom - should be the first aider or senior member of staff.

The circumstances of the accident, and any adults and children involved and any witnesses.

The signature of the staff member who dealt with the accident, any witnesses and countersigned by the parent when the child is collected.

Dealing with dilemmas

A child of three who has a severe allergy to nuts attends your nursery. The parent has advised you of this, and given you strict instructions about what the child should not come into contact with in your setting - just being near to anything containing nut oil could bring on an anaphylactic shock reaction. What measures do you need to have in place to help this child?

This is one of the hardest situations for any carer, in any setting, to deal with. Many foods contain nut oil that you may not know about - be guided by the parent in the first instance, and make sure that you have a clear agreement about the treatment the child will need to receive if the child becomes unwell.

How would you recognise the effects of nut allergy?

If there was a mild reaction, you would see the child become sick, or show signs of a rash in a particular area of their body. If nuts have been near to the child's mouth, the child may feel a tingling sensation in their mouth. These symptoms may not seem too serious. However, a more serious reaction may occur at any time. A severe reaction to nuts could show within minutes of a child being in contact with nuts or nut oil found in different foods. The child may have an anaphylactic shock - treatment in the form of an Epipen will need to be used immediately, perhaps to save the child's life. At least one member of staff trained in the use of the Epipen should always be on the premises. Health visitors may be asked to offer this training. It is advisable for each setting to explore this subject, to be comfortable about dealing with this condition.

Further information

The Anaphylaxis Campaign, PO Box 27, Farnborough, Hampshire GU14 6SX
Tel: 01252 542029   Fax: 01252 377140
Or visit the website: www.nutallergy.net

Sick children

A sick child will be unsettled and perhaps frightened. One person should care for the child until either the parent arrives, or an ambulance. The child will need to be given plenty of love and reassurance. This is a care issue - imagine yourself as a child who is not feeling well or injured. How would you wish to be treated?

You should have clear policies and procedures about how to deal with a sick child. The documents should show the system you have in place to contact parents - are your contact details up to date? Do you have emergency contact numbers? Check regularly with the parents that the contact numbers are correct. Do you have a sick room or quiet area for a sick child? This is important if the child has an infectious illness that you are trying to contain.

Smoking

Smoking should not be allowed in group settings, and parents and staff should be aware of this through a written policy. This is an issue for childminders - the guidance book for them states that a childminder may smoke in the presence of children, with parental agreement. This is considered in detail in the following section for Standard 7, for childminders.

Good practice

■ Encourage children to understand about good health.

■ Spend time with the children on topics related to health - teeth, food, exercise, overcoming fears of going to the doctor/dentist/hospital.

■ Use the home corner imaginatively to promote healthy living.

■ Allow the children to tidy up, and clean - they enjoy this, when they are young!

■ Make good use of your newsletters to advise parents on current health issues, such as head lice or conjunctivitis - when a child is not ill, but should be at home until treatment has been given.

■ Think about how parents can get involved - do any of your parents work in a health environment? If so, enlist their help.

■ Invite health professionals to your setting to be involved with children directly.

What will the inspector be looking for?

Accident records - *written evidence*

Medication or emergency treatment forms - *written evidence*

Medication records - *written evidence*

First aid box(es) - *visual evidence*

Your arrangements for sick children - *verbal discussion*

Written agreements concerning smoking - *written evidence - policies*

The standard to be reached:
The registered person promotes the good health of children and takes positive steps to prevent the spread of infection and appropriate measures when they are ill.

Requirements that you must comply with: Children Act regulations
You must keep a record of all medicines administered to children.

You must keep a signed record of all accidents to children, and notify Ofsted of any serious injury or death to any child in your care.

You must notify Ofsted of any infectious diseases that a qualified medical person considers notifiable.

A childminder is solely responsible for the healthy environment that is their home. Unlike in a group setting, a childminder has to consider the following points for themselves:

Hygiene in the home

Your own standards with your own family are your starting point, but when you are responsible for other people's children, you may need to consider other issues. The registration course you will have attended will have given you information about what you need to consider. Remember, you are under agreement to the parents to care for their children. The parents would expect a clean environment, with equipment in good repair. Your own hygiene practice should be good - you are setting an example to the children when they see you wash your hands, keep your hair tidy, and present yourself well. Children will pick up good, and bad, habits.

Pets/animals the children may come into contact with

Many parents are pleased to leave their children with a childminder who has pets, as it may be that they are unable to have pets themselves. You are responsible for ensuring the children's safety in every respect in your home - never leave the children with your pets unsupervised. Your usually docile dog may be having a bad day, and turn on the child who wants to play. Cats may scratch a child who comes too near. Most childminders consider health issues with their pets, and make sure that children wash hands regularly when the pets have been in contact with the child. This should apply too, if you take the children out on a visit to anywhere that animals can be found.

Equipment - the sandpit

Your sandpit should be kept covered when not in use - cats will use them as a toilet. Clean the sand regularly and sieve it. Let the children help - a great activity!

Food handling

The environmental health department is a useful contact if you need to ask anything about health matters related to your home. A food handling course is probably the best way to learn about the safe preparation and cooking of food. This is far more than cleaning the surfaces well, and washing your hands regularly.

It may be that you do not cook a main meal for the children, but at some stage you will be offering snacks and drinks - the correct temperature for storing food is something you could find out about through a course, or by accessing the written information from the environmental health department.

Medication, the first aid kit and the sick child

You should have accident records alongside your first aid kit, so that you are able to write the report as soon as you have dealt with the injured child. You could also make a note if you are running low of any items for the first aid kit - always keep the first aid box full. The items you use for your own family should be kept separately. Always seek advice from the parents on emergency matters - keep the contact numbers of parents by your phone, and take the numbers with you when you take the children out.

It may be that a child in your care has attended pre-school in the morning and had an accident there. You would be asked to sign for this - make sure that the parent is told of the accident, and given a copy of the signed form, too.

If you are asked to give a child medication, make sure it is prescribed and that the child is well enough to be with you - the decision is yours. You need to judge if the child would be better off at home. The parents may be unhappy about your decision, but you have to think about yourself, and the other children. This issue could be agreed when you first meet, and are agreeing the wording on your contract.

Smoking

Most childminders would not smoke in the area that young children are being cared for and feel that, as professional carers, they should have the same guidance as for group carers. This issue is being taken forward by the National Childminding Association (NCMA), who feel strongly about the health issues for children in the care of childminders. The difficulty that childminders are faced with is in respect of parents who do not object to you smoking in their child's presence, and the parents who would not want you to do this. The chances are, you will be caring for children from more than one family. Common sense, and your own professional knowledge, provide you with the answer. Discuss the issue with parents and say, if you are a smoker, 'I do smoke, but recognise that there are health issues for your child if I smoke in front of them. I have chosen not to smoke when your children are present'. It would be surprising if all the parents did not appreciate this.

The National Standards are due to be reviewed in 2003. It is hoped by many that the review will include discussion over the issues raised about childminders and smoking, to recognise the obvious health issues for young children.

Food and drink

The standard to be reached:
Children are provided with regular drinks and food in adequate quantities for their needs. Food and drink is properly prepared, nutritious and complies with dietary and religious requirements.

What does this mean for your setting?
Promoting healthy eating patterns is difficult today, when so many children are in day care settings. Children may have meals or snacks at home, nursery, pre-school or out-of-school club. It may be that a packed lunch is provided for the children by the parents, or breakfast, lunch and tea is provided by the setting. Staff must recognise that children have different dietary or cultural needs. Menus should reflect this.

What do you need to do?
There are two main areas under this standard that need to be addressed. You need to consider criteria points 8.1 - 8.4.

Drinking water
It may seem obvious to say that children should be offered water throughout the day/session. However, it is surprising how many settings do not have water available to the children for when they ask for it, or just have it ready in jugs or bottles. Do the children know that they can have a drink whenever they want one? Thirst is not a comfortable feeling. Why should water, in particular, be offered? Water will quench a child's thirst and will not damage teeth. Some drinks are filling, and may affect a child's appetite. This does not mean that children should never be offered other drinks, but water offers the healthy choice as a drink to quench thirst - encourage children to help themselves if possible. Tap water is suitable for children. Many people now buy bottled water, but it has a higher level of salts, and may therefore not be suitable for young children. Other points to remember in respect of water are:

■ Temperature

Children will need more refreshments on a hot day - keep water cool and offer it regularly to the children.

■ Illness

A child may need to drink more if they are unwell.

Remember - recognise each child as an individual, and meet the child's needs.

Meals
You should offer interesting, nutritious meals to the children in your care. This is easier said than done if you are to meet individual needs. How can you do this?

Think about the meals you are able to provide. Whatever setting you work in, at some time during the day you will need to offer a snack, a main meal, more than one meal, treats, or you may be overseeing the children eat a packed lunch prepared by the parents. Consider the situation where you are providing three meals a day, in other words, offering full day care. You are responsible for ensuring that all dietary needs are met for the children each day - this will have an important effect on the child's health, and how eating habits will be formed.

Food should be nutritious. What do we mean by a nutritious diet for young children? In *A Practical Guide to Child Nutrition* by Angela Dare and Margaret O'Donovan (Stanley Thornes, ISBN 0 7487 2375 7) the authors state: 'Nutrients are the

building blocks' of food which carry out the following functions:

■ providing warmth and energy to maintain body temperature and keep all organs and muscles working properly;

■ providing new material for growth;

■ maintaining and renewing body tissues;

■ keeping all the body processes, including the prevention of infection, in good order.

There are seven essential nutrients: proteins, carbohydrates, fats, vitamins, minerals, fibre and water. They each have a part to play in the growth and health of the body.

What is a varied diet? There are four main groups of food that need to be considered when you are meeting a child's dietary needs.
These are:

Bread, cereals and potatoes

Fruit and vegetables

Milk and dairy foods

Meat and fish

Remember, too, the vegetarian alternatives, such as pulses and soya. If a parent tells you that their child is vegetarian (not eating meat or fish), or vegan (not eating foods of animal origin (meat, fish and dairy produce), you will have a challenge to ensure that the child still has a balanced and nutritious diet to enable healthy development. You will need to be guided by the parents on what the child may and may not eat. When menus are planned, use the information given to you by the parents. or, if possible, involve the children in making choices for the menu. It may be that the children have been involved in a cooking activity to provide the food for the snack or tea. Do you allow the children to be involved at mealtimes in the following ways?

- Laying the table.

- Counting how many children will need chairs/highchairs.

- Older children acting as monitors, taking the snack around the table, offering to each child, and expecting a word of thanks.

Staff involvement

Do the staff consider the mealtime or snack time to be a social time with the children?

Do staff sit with children at tables and talk to them, or do they stand to one side with a cup of coffee making their own conversation? As a parent, which would you prefer to see?

Are meals served at the table, with staff asking children how much they would like to eat? Are second helpings offered?

Are the tables laid attractively? Some settings have tablecloths, and small vases of fresh flowers in the centre, manageable jugs of water for the children to help themselves and table placemats that the children have made for themselves for their own place.

Do staff feed the children, or encourage independent use of appropriate cutlery?

Parents

Clearly, the dietary information you need about each child will come from the parents. You need to respect children's feelings about likes and dislikes of certain foods, but also recognise that they may feel different if the meal they are offered is not the same as the other children's. How can you overcome this? Could you offer all the children a vegetarian meal, for example, once a week? Have you considered cultural differences? To include a varied and interesting diet to reflect other cultures is good for all the children.

In *Eating Well for the Under Fives in Childcare* (Caroline Walker Trust, ISBN 1 897820 07 0) there is useful information to help you in recognising food to celebrate festivals throughout the year.

There are several good books available about cooking for children in general. Your local bookseller will have a range to choose from - look specifically for those that consider meal planning, such as *The Baby and Toddler Meal Planner* by Anna Carmel (Ebury Press, ISBN 0 09 186360 0). The meals may be targeted at younger children, but they will give you inspiration for the older children, too!

How do all the staff know about each child's dietary needs? The parents will have advised the manager/supervisor of the setting of any specific needs when the child starts with you. The person preparing the meals should have a list of children in the kitchen area, showing

•••••••••••••••••••••••••••••
SHAP calendar of religious festivals
SHAP Working Party
c/o National Society RE Centre
Church House
Great Smith Street
London SW1P 3NZ
Tel: 020 7898 1494
•••••••••••••••••••••••••••••

special dietary or cultural requirements. The child's key worker, or staff responsible for the children in the room, should also be made aware of each child's dietary needs, and discuss this openly with the parents. Staff are not expected to have a full understanding of all dietary matters - this is very much a part of working with parents, and asking for information from them. The best policy is to be honest - if you don't know, say so! Parents will be happy to advise you on the best diet for their child - learn from this, and even ask for recipes that you could use. This would be an excellent example of good practice in working with the parents, and you would also be ensuring that you meet the child's dietary needs.

If parents provide lunchboxes for their children, you need to be careful. It may be that the child can only eat specific foods. Children need observing, as they will tend to help themselves to others food, particularly if it seems better than theirs! A member of staff should always

Dealing with dilemmas

You are working in a nursery in the room where children aged three to five years are cared for. One male child, who has been with you for a short time, has a weight problem. Today, you overheard another child call him 'fatty'. The boy became upset and started crying. What can you do about this situation?

There may be a medical reason why the child is overweight. Children can be cruel at times, and not realise that they have hurt someone's feelings by calling them names. This particular issue can be dealt with as a larger group, when you talk to the children about 'How we feel when...'. This will enable all children to understand that everyone has feelings, and we should all try to make everyone feel good about themselves.

Staff should act as positive role models, by offering praise to the children for all their efforts and building self-esteem. A child with a medical condition that results in them becoming overweight needs much support from staff. Children need to be aware that we all have differences, and will have different strengths, too. Staff should promote each child's strengths in the setting.

A child who is overweight because of poor eating habits can be helped in other ways. It may be that the family would welcome some guidance in this area. How could you deal with this issue, without focusing on one family? The answer lies in your planning for topics. You can call the topic 'Ourselves' and plan to cover a number of issues that affect everyone, such as:

> How we grow
>
> Food that helps us to grow
>
> How we look after ourselves
>
> Teeth
>
> Hair

Your home corner could become the local fruit and vegetable shop, and you could invite a variety of professional people/parents to visit the setting to talk to the children about a number of issues relating to food. Some settings invite people in to do cooking with children, and talk to them about healthy ways to cook.

For some families, finances are stretched. Sadly, many cheaper foods, which provide energy, are the main diet, whereas foods necessary for children's development, such as fruit and vegetables, are more expensive. If you can think of ways in which to help parents on a budget to look at the healthier options, you will be helping the children, too. You can also provide more opportunities for children to get exercise through your planning for physical development. Children will join in if you make games fun, and allow all children to achieve at some stage.

be seated at the table to ensure that children with food from home eat only that food. Be advised by the environmental health officer on the storage of lunchboxes, particularly for holiday playschemes, if no fridges or cold store room is available. You may need to ask parents to place ice packs in the lunchboxes to keep the food cold.

Good practice

■ Children need to eat regularly. Whenever it is possible, try to keep to a child's own routine for meals.

■ Babies who are bottle fed should be held and have warm physical contact with the adult during feed times.

■ Parents should be advised daily if the child has not eaten the meals provided that day – and advised of any amounts left.

■ Allow time for children to eat - children need to be encouraged to eat slowly, as this is better for the digestive system.

■ Make mealtimes a social time. If possible, staff should eat and drink with the children, to set a good example. If staff have separate meal breaks, they should still sit with the children at the table, and talk to them.

■ Encourage good table manners.

■ Children should go to the toilet and wash their hands before sitting to the table.

■ Children under five years should not be left alone whilst they eat, in case they choke.

■ Store food correctly. Do not leave perishable food at room temperatures for more than two hours.

Remember - the environmental health department is available for advice.

What will the inspector be looking for?

Children's records indicating their dietary needs - *booking forms and kitchen area*

Your arrangements for providing food and drink - *menus and written policies*

How you find out about and meet children's dietary needs - *verbal discussion*

The arrangements you make when parents provide food and drink for their child - *verbal discussion, named lunchboxes, fridge or cold store available. Ice packs requested from parents. Staff sit with children at mealtimes.*

The standard to be met:
Children are provided with regular drinks and food in adequate quantities for their needs. Food and drink is properly prepared, nutritious and complies with dietary requirements.

You need to consider criteria points 8.1 - 8.3.

When you are shopping for food and drink, you need to consider not only the needs of your own children but the needs of the minded children, too. Some childminders keep a separate basket for the childminding food (for the purposes of having a receipt).

Should the food differ in any way to the food you are buying for your family? The answer is probably 'yes'. Your own family will have their likes and dislikes, and you will take this into account when you shop. Equally, your minded children may have specific dietary needs/preferences. You will have discussed this with the parents, and agreed on the food to be given to the child. This is likely to have been agreed in writing, in your contract with the parents.

An issue that usually arises is that of sweets and treats. You will, at some time, be taking the children out to the local shop, and the children may ask you for sweets. A good tip is to stick to one day of the week when you will treat the children - agree this with the parents first. Children will then come to understand that you only buy sweets on this one day. Be consistent in your approach - it does work!

Drinking water should be available to the children at all times. If possible, keep a jug of cool water ready to give to the children on request, or to help themselves as they get older. If you are out in the garden on a hot day, remember that the children will need refreshment, as well as yourself. Be prepared, take what you need outside with you, as you may not be able to go back indoors without taking all the children with you, for example, if the paddling pool is out.

Think about healthy and nutritious snacks for the children - offer them food regularly. Allow children to help you prepare meals/snacks. Above all, regularly discuss the children's dietary needs with the parents. Children's needs change as they get older.

Equal opportunities

The standard to be reached:
The registered person and staff actively promote equality of opportunity and anti-discriminatory practice for all children.

This standard on its own seems simple enough to address. However, equal opportunity should be linked to each National Standard, demanding a deeper understanding of the issues by staff working in your setting.

What does this mean for your setting?

You need to consider criteria points 9.1 - 9.3 in some detail. Firstly, and most importantly, think about what the term 'equal opportunities' means. If you were to ask this question, many would reply 'Well, it means to treat everyone the same'. This response is understandable - if you treat everyone in the same way, you are not treating anyone differently, and this must be fair. Or is it?

Think about the effect this would have on the children in your care. If you were to treat children in exactly the same way, that is, to give the same toys to all the children, the same food, and expect the same level of work from them, what difficulties could there be for them?

The answer lies in the word 'same'. You need to think of each child as an individual, not as part of a group that is given the same as everyone else.

■ You need to consider choice of the range of toys and play materials you have in your setting.

■ You need to consider food preferences/allergies when you are putting together your menus.

■ You need to consider each child in terms of their age/developmental stage when planning your curriculum or programme.

What do you need to do?

Equal opportunities needs to be considered for the children, the staff and the parents. In this way, you will be able to show how you respect everyone, regardless of their circumstances. Rather than think about equal opportunities as a standard on its own, think of the issues running like a thread throughout all of the standards you need to reach.

Policies and procedures

These documents are considered in more detail under Standard 14 (Documentation) in this book. Your policies and procedures are a clear statement of how you approach the care of the children in your setting. The key to a well-worded policy on equal opportunity is how you explain what you mean by treating all children according to their individual needs.

Explain - that you recognise that all children develop at their own pace, and that your curriculum has been planned to enable all children to develop to their potential.

Explain - that you recognise the importance of involving parents in the forming of the policy document.

Explain - that you intend to develop in the children a real sense of belonging in the community/society, recognising cultural differences, and celebrating them.

Explain - that you are committed to promoting our diverse society in a positive way.

Explain - that you encourage your staff to attend training on issues relating to inclusion, to give them an even greater understanding of the issues they face in caring for young children in today's world.

Explain - how you will put the policy into practice. This will mean giving an explanation of your procedures that staff follow to implement the written policy. Under Standard 14, suggestions on how you can achieve this are given (see pages 60-63).

In most settings, policies and procedures are written in English, yet the families you work with may not speak or understand English. It could be costly to have all your documents printed in other languages, so how can you deal with this? If you are working in an area where there are many families who, for example, speak Urdu, it may seem sensible to arrange for your documents to be written in Urdu for that community. But what about the one child who is, for example, Chinese? These are difficulties that some settings face. The best way to deal with this is to think practically about the issues.

■ Do you have a welcome poster, displayed in the entrance, to offer a greeting to everyone, regardless of the language barriers?

■ Do you have a contact within your local education service that could put you in contact with an interpreter, for the families that will have difficulties in communicating with the staff?

■ Do the staff feel confident in challenging inappropriate comments?

■ Does your book selection reflect our diverse society?

- Do your pictures and posters show positive images of male and female roles, people of different colours and abilities?

All of these strategies, and others that you may have already put in place, will demonstrate how you think of each family and child as individual, recognising their needs, and promoting their language/cultural differences in a positive way.

It must be stressed that equal opportunities is not just about the colour of skin - there are wider issues for everyone to consider:

- Language

- Ability

- Age

- Cultures and beliefs

Encourage your staff to attend any training that will enable them to learn about other people's cultures and beliefs.

Anti-discriminatory good practice

What does this mean? We need to think about those people who are regularly discriminated against in today's society. They may include older people, people with white or black skin, large people, small people, individuals with a physical disability, those for whom English is a second language, gifted people, gay and lesbian people - the list goes on, because at some time in everyone's life, there is a feeling that 'I do not get a fair chance in society. This is because I am...'. We all, at some stage, are not satisfied with, for example, our appearance, work efforts, communication skills and so on. To then hear unkind comments about this is not good for our feelings, so imagine how a child may feel in a similar situation.

Each child needs to feel that they are a part of your setting, a part of their peer group, a part of the local community. The child should be encouraged to share experiences within the group - introduce a news time, so that all children can share their special news with everyone,

Dealing with dilemmas

You work in a setting that is in a predominantly white area. You have never cared for a child whose first language is not English, and who is not white. A parent, Mrs Smith, is visiting today with her three-year-old son, Peter. You have not met before, and are looking forward to showing the parent and child what you offer in terms of quality care and education. You open the door. Mrs Smith and Peter are black, and you are taken by surprise. What are the issues here?

You had assumed, with Smith and Peter being fairly common English names, that the family would be white. In fact, Mrs Smith has moved to this country and married a white Englishman, and the choice of name for their son was mutually agreed.

Never assume the colour of skin by the name you hear.

If you are honest, what resources do you have to represent the whole society? You work in an area where all families are white. Have you ensured that the children in your care gain a broader understanding of the wider community, in terms of cultures, beliefs, colour and language? This does not just mean a tokenistic approach of placing a black doll in the home corner, a few books showing various people from around the world, and the welcome poster in the entrance hall.

It is even more important in predominantly white areas for children to understand about other people beyond their immediate community. The attitude of the staff to equal opportunity issues needs to be positive. Children learn attitudes from the people around them.

Think about your resources and ask for ideas/information from your support worker about how you can positively promote all sections of society in your setting, all the time, not just when a black family arrives at your setting.

for example, what they did at the weekend, news about a baby brother or sister being born, information about their pets. This will build children's self-esteem, and encourage them to explore their feelings. A wall chart showing faces with different expressions is an excellent way of helping children to talk about their feelings in a non-threatening way.

What play resources are available for each child? Do you consider providing a wide range range of toys and play materials for boys and girls, reflecting our multicultural society? Are they all available to all the children, regardless of age, gender, ability? Importantly, do your play activities enable children to gain some understanding of other people's views?

Many settings state that they value diversity. If this is written into your policy,

is there an understanding of what the term means? There is no point in writing policies that the staff cannot explain. For staff to recognise the importance of respect for other people's ways of life, and not be judgmental about those choices, is a key factor in how this standard can be met in your setting.

Information to parents

More than your written policies and procedures, think about your verbal communication with parents. Telling parents about your setting and changes that may be occurring are the usual examples of what you discuss. However, parents need to know personally about:

- Who will be caring for their child - how you manage a key worker system, or other system

- Who needs to know of the child's dietary, medical or cultural needs

- How you keep the children safe

Parents need to be able to inform you about:

- The child's current routine - sleeping patterns, for example

- Special toys (comforters), food preferences or allergies

- Any difficulties, such as special educational needs.

Some parents may not speak English, or be able to read your policy and procedures documents. Consider how you will be able to help these people to have a good understanding of how your setting operates. The language barrier could be overcome with the help of an interpreter, and for people who are unable to read, verbal explanations will be necessary. If a parent is embarrassed to tell you that they are unable to read, you may never know, which is why it is important to give verbal as well as written information to all parents.

Good practice

- It is useful for the registered person and staff to have training in areas of inclusion and relevant legislation. The registered person may not always be on site, but they should still have a clear understanding of the issues relating to this standard. There is legislation linked to this area, and the training can keep you up to date on the changes as they affect you. Joint training between registered providers and staff is also good for working relationships.

- Review your resources to reflect the wider community. Use the library for information, ask members of the community, parents and professional people in to talk to the children or do an activity with them.

- Make sure that all children have equal access to all play materials - encourage the children to consider each other, explore feelings, and build their self-

esteem. Never underestimate the importance of imaginative play opportunities.

- What thought have you given to your admissions policy? You should be clear about how children are admitted to your setting, and what criteria need to be met for admission, for example, the age of the child, if you make exceptions to your waiting list (siblings). Decisions on admission should be thought of in terms of equal access for all.

- Do you have a recruitment and employment policy or statement in place for staff? The wording of this should reflect that you are an equal opportunities employer. Your local support worker will help you with the wording of such a document, or you could contact the Advisory, Conciliation and Arbitration Service (ACAS), 27 Wilton Street, London SW16 4ER. Tel: 0208 679 8000.

What will the inspector be looking for?
Children's records - *written evidence*

Your equal opportunities policy - *written evidence, and verbal explanation of understanding of the issues for your setting*

How you comply with relevant legislation - *certificates of attendance to training, verbal comment on where you accessed the information, and how you have applied this to the setting*

How you find out about children's specific needs - *through your verbal discussion with parents, and information written down from that discussion. Written information from parents, for example, on a booking form, admission form.*

The standard to be reached:
The registered person and staff actively promote equality of opportunity and anti-discriminatory practice for all children.

When you care for other people's children in your own home, there are many ways in which you can consider treating the children with equal concern. To value each child as an individual, and allow access to a wide range of play opportunities, seems a simple way of explaining the term 'treat with equal concern'. How will you achieve this in your home, when you have your own cultures/beliefs to consider, in addition to meeting the needs of your own family?

Firstly, you need to think about the information you receive from the parents about their child, to be certain that you can meet the child's needs. Many childminders are concerned that they may appear not to be considering equal opportunity if they do not take on a child, for example, with a disability. Let's look at this issue.

You may be approached to care for a child who needs to use a wheelchair. Is your home suitable for this - can the wheelchair fit through your door? Do you live in a first floor flat? These are valid reasons to not take on the care of the child - your premises are not suitable. It may be that you consider that you can help this family, but the effect on the other children in your care will need to be thought about. Only by having a trial period will you know that an arrangement can become permanent.

There can be no reason to not take on a child from a family whose skin colour is different to your own.

Some children have a special need that you may have to consider - many childminders are able to accommodate children with difficulties in their homes, and find this work rewarding.

All children should be treated with

equal concern. How can you, as a childminder, demonstrate this? Think firstly about the child as an individual, who needs you for what you can offer. Think about the following:

Children need to:

- have stable relationships with their carers

- have familiar routines

- have access to favourite comfort toys, such as their teddy

- have respect

- have a sense of belonging

- hear words of praise and encouragement

- become increasingly independent

- have consistent attitudes from their carers

- understand right from wrong

- develop skills

  - have an awareness of themselves and others

  - be able to express feelings

  - develop relationships with their peers

If you consider that you give each child in your care these opportunities, and others you may think of, you will be recognising each child individually.

You are not expected to know about every type of condition, medical need or special educational need of every child. Discussion with the parents, and asking for further information through libraries or through your support worker, will enrich your knowledge and enable you to work well with the families you come into contact with.

Special needs

The standard to be reached (including special educational needs and disabilities):
The registered person is aware that some children may have special needs and is proactive in ensuring that appropriate action can be taken when such a child is identified or admitted to the provision. Steps are taken to promote the welfare and development of the child within the setting in partnership with the parents and other relevant parties.

Before we consider how you could reach the standard, you need to be clear about what is meant by the term 'special needs'.

In many settings, if carers were to be asked about children with special needs, the response would probably include reference to the Special Educational Needs Code of Practice, which should be in every setting. This book relates mainly to children in the Foundation Stage, aged between three and six.

However, the term 'special needs' can refer to a child with special care needs, such as a dietary need or a care need related to a physical disability.

Special *educational* needs are not the same. For example, you may be caring for a child who needs additional help in terms of their learning. The child may be having greater difficulty in learning than most children of a similar age and will need support to be able to progress.

Many people would consider all children to be special which, of course, they are. However, some children are special for specific reasons. The term would perhaps indicate that a child is in need of extra help, either with respect to a medical condition - a physical disability, for example - or in terms of their educational and/or social development.

What does this mean for your setting?

It may be that a child is placed in your setting because you specialise in helping children with certain difficulties. Staff may be trained in meeting the needs of, for example, children with cerebral palsy. For most settings - creches, pre-schools, nurseries, out-of-school clubs and holiday clubs - children attend with no obvious concerns. It may be that, through your observations, you identify a need for a child, which has not been picked up on previously. This is a sensitive issue, as the parents will need to be approached in a sympathetic way. Some parents may find it hard to accept that their child has a special care or educational need. Some could be in denial of the situation and you may need help from an outside agency or other professionals.

A child with a special care or educational need is likely to come under one or more of the following categories:

Learning difficulty

Sensory impairment

Speech and language problems

Physical disability

Behavioural/social/communication/interaction problems

Medical/dietary/cultural

A gifted child may also have a special need. It is widely recognised that some gifted children can have difficulties relating to their peers and may, for example, need help in developing their social skills. Not many settings would think the gifted child needed additional support, as it is more often thought that children with difficulties are the ones who need extra support to progress. Support for all children with special needs, including those who are gifted, needs to be considered. Think about the following:

- What information do you have about the child?

- Can you help this child, and support the family?

- Does your policy statement reflect your commitment to support all families?

- Have you considered the access to your premises? Access to play materials/equipment?

- Do all of the staff have knowledge of the Code of Practice – identification and assessment of special educational needs in the Foundation Stage?

- Are regular observations carried out on children individually, as well as within group activity times?

- Are all children included?

These issues concern all children and their families. However, regard should be given to all children who need extra help, whether this is because of a care need or an educational need.

Under Standard 6 (Safety), we considered the importance of risk assessment. There is a link to this standard, as some children with special needs may have no understanding of personal or group safety.

The Code of Practice
The Code of Practice is a large book, with much information for you to take on board. Within each local authority there is a SENCO - special educational needs co-ordinator - who is there to support all Foundation Stage settings. You should also appoint a named SENCO in your setting to be the contact for the local authority area SENCO.

So, what is the Code of Practice, and how does it apply to your setting?

There are some organisations listed in the back of your guidance books, which are helpful contacts for you in meeting this standard. These include:

Centre for Accessible Environments
Nutmeg House
60 Gainsford Street
London SE1 2NY
Tel: 0207 357 8182
Website: www.cae.org.uk

National Association of Toy and Leisure Libraries (NATLL)
68 Churchway
London NW1 1LT
Tel: 0207 387 9592
Website: www.natll.org.uk

If your setting does not have a copy of the Code of Practice, revised edition, you should contact:

Department for Education and Skills (DfES) Publications
PO Box 5050
Sherwood Park
Annesley
Nottingham NG15 0DJ
Tel: 0845 6022260
Website: www.dfes.gov.uk

Five fundamental principles of the Code of Practice are:

- A child with special needs should have their needs met.

- The special educational needs of children will normally be met in settings.

- The view of the child should be sought and taken into account.

- Parents have a vital role to play in supporting their child's education.

- Children with special educational needs should be offered full access to a broad, balanced and relevant education, including an appropriate curriculum for the

Foundation Stage and the National Curriculum.

Chapter 4 of the Code of Practice gives details about the following:

- Provision in the early years

- Graduated response – monitoring of individual children's progress

- The role of the SENCO

- Individual records

- Early Years Action

- Individual educational plans

- Requests for statutory assessment

- Statutory assessment of children under compulsory school age

- Children under two years

- Moving to primary school

Advice on the implications of the Code of Practice for your setting can be sought through your support worker – your area SENCO within your local authority. As the registered person, you need to ensure that you have a SEN policy in place. The person who you appoint as your SENCO for the setting may ask for staff training so that everyone is aware of procedures that will need to be in place for identifying, assessing and supporting children with special educational needs.

The Foundation Stage - children aged three to six

Since January 2002, all early years settings are expected to have regard for the Code of Practice. Each setting should have appointed a SENCO, who will have agreed to train in identifying and

managing special educational needs. Two stages of action and intervention to be considered are:

Early Years Action – the initial concerns

These may be noted by parents, health visitors or staff in your setting:

- Makes little or no progress, even when staff have used approaches that target the difficulties;

- Continues to work at a level well below that expected of a child of similar age;

- Displays persistent emotional and/or behavioural difficulties despite the strategies staff may have used to address this;

- Has sensory or physical problems and makes little or no progress despite the personal aids or equipment being made available to them;

- Has communication difficulties and needs specific support in order to learn.

Early Years Action Plus – when the initial concerns continue

It is noted that the child:

- Continues to make little or no progress over a long period of time;

- Continues to work within the curriculum well below that of his or her peers;

- Continues to experience emotional and/or behavioural difficulties;

- Will need specialist equipment with regular support from a specialist practitioner;

- Continues to have communication problems that affect social development and learning.

From initial observations, staff may consider that the child may need some additional help or support. You are not expected to be an expert in the field of special needs. You are expected, however, to put policies and procedures in place to show how the additional help and support will be accessed.

Remember, the parents must be involved in any process you put into place.

Good practice

- Staff should recognise that there are care needs and educational needs. For example, a child who is diabetic has a specific care need but not a special educational need. A child who is gifted intellectually or bilingual may have a special or additional need but would not be considered to have a special educational need. Staff should be confident in their knowledge of child development.

- Make sure that your staff know about the Special Educational Needs Code of Practice book, where it is kept, and the procedures you have in place for the identification, assessment and support for children who need additional help. Staff should know where to go for help for children with specific needs, too. Your local support worker can help with this.

- Encourage your staff to go on training courses to further their knowledge in this area.

- Your named SENCO should attend training, to gain an understanding of any legislation that applies to your setting.

- Think about your physical environment – is it suitable for all the children who attend your setting? Do you consider the space for each child to have access to all toys and equipment?

- Are staff comfortable in writing observations on children? It is not good enough to write 'Child had a good day'. This tells you nothing, except perhaps that the child was settled. If a member of staff noted a problem, could they record this in a way that would not cause unnecessary alarm for the parents? This could be a training issue.

- Do the staff in your setting have positive attitudes to the care of the children - do they act as good role models, treat the children with respect and communicate with them? Do they think about the way in which they deal with children's behaviour, using a firm but fair approach? Are they consistent in care management?

- Staff working in your setting are subject to issues of confidentiality, only sharing information about a child with the permission of the parents, if there is a concern about the child's development.

- Inclusion seems to be the main consideration for settings. There are a number of ways you can consider this. A positive attitude from everyone connected to your setting is the main point. Within your resources, do you provide the children with positive images of the whole of our society, including those with differing abilities?

Dealing with dilemmas

A three-year-old boy attends your pre-school who is lively - always on the go. He prefers to run around rather than sit at a table and join in an activity. He is loud and boisterous, and has little concentration. He has, with a couple of the other boys, found a route around the room and runs around at every opportunity. You are concerned about the child's behaviour, and think that perhaps there is a problem because he has so little concentration. You ask your support worker for advice.

- The support worker arrives at your setting to observe the child. This is good, as you now have another person from outside to look at the situation from a different perspective.

- The support worker notices that as well as the boy running around the room, there are a couple of girls, too, but they are not so noisy. The staff had not noticed this - they had focused on the boys, one in particular, who is louder than the others.

- The support worker can see how the room has been planned, in terms of layout of furniture and equipment. It is clear that the children have found it easy to make a route to run around in the setting.

The advice given is that the child is three years of age. It is usual for three-year-olds to be boisterous. The child is naturally energetic, and this is not a problem - you can channel his energies in different ways.

Allow a time for the children to burn off their energy, but have quieter times when the children do not run around. Your routine or plans should allow for quiet and noisy times. Moving the furniture to restrict the route that has been made for running will help with this.

It is easy to think that the child has a problem - he lacks concentration. But how much effort have the staff put into encouraging the child to participate in other activities? Do your staff act as good role models, sitting at the tables, involved with the activities on offer?

The child is louder than others. Is that why it was not so noticeable that girls as well as boys were involved in the running games?

It may be that, on another occasion, your support worker observes a child and agrees with you that the child may have a difficulty. Before you ask for a visit from your support worker, think about the comments above - there could be things that you could do to help a child.

What will the inspector be looking for?

Children's records – *written evidence and verbal discussion*

Your written statement about special needs – *written evidence*

Your arrangements for caring for children with special needs – *verbal discussion*

How you share information about your provision for children with special needs with parents – *your policies and procedures, and verbal discussion*

The standard to be reached:

The registered person is aware that some children may have special needs and is proactive in ensuring that appropriate action can be taken when such a child is identified or admitted to the provision. Steps are taken to promote the welfare and development of the child within the setting in partnership with the parents and other relevant parties.

The previous section, for group care, will help you in understanding what is meant by the term 'special needs'. Special needs may be described as care needs or educational needs.

As a childminder, you need to be aware of the identification of children who may have special needs. This does not mean that you need to be an expert, but you do need to know enough about child development to be able to recognise when a child may need additional help. If you are to consider confidentiality, where can you ask for help? It may be that you would prefer to discuss this with a professional, before you speak to the parents. This is understandable, as it is a sensitive subject to raise with parents. No one likes to hear that their child may have problems. Equally, though, most parents would prefer to know at the earliest point in time, so that appropriate help can be given to the child.

Your local support worker, network co-ordinator, local authority area SENCO or health visitor may be able to help you in approaching the parents, and suggesting ways in which you can help a child with difficulties.

It may be that you have been approached by a parent to care for their child with, for example, learning difficulties. You need to consider this carefully in a home setting. You have your family to consider, and the other children in your care. Most childminders give good thought to helping a family with a child who may have behavioural problems, and will offer a temporary contract to see how the child settles into the home. This would be the same process for any child you are to care for. If you know from the start that you would not be able to meet the child's needs, it would be better to state this immediately to the parent, suggesting that the child would perhaps be more suited to another setting, where their needs could be met. Childminders who are able to help families with children who are experiencing difficulties will agree that the work is hard but rewarding. Some childminders have found that their own children have enriched knowledge of others through this contact within their home, and learn tolerance and understanding from a young age.

Your relationships with the parents are professional, but friendly, and you should always work to support the families you come into contact with as a registered childminder.

If you are unaware of the Code of Practice and how this affects your work, contact your local education department and ask for the area SENCO to advise you on what you need to know. If you need advice on a care need, your initial discussion will be with the parents. Further help is available through your local support worker.

Behaviour

The standard to be reached:
Adults caring for children in the provision are able to manage a wide range of children's behaviour in a way which promotes their welfare and development.

The focus for this standard, which is written under the bold print in your guidance book, is helpful. It says:

'Children benefit most where adults adopt a consistent and positive approach to the management of their behaviour. By establishing clear boundaries according to the child's level of understanding, children become aware of the setting's routines and procedures and know what is expected of them.'

What does this mean for your setting?
The key words for this standard are:

- Adults - promote children's welfare and development
- Adopt a consistent and positive approach
- Establish clear boundaries
- Children - know what is expected of them

You need to consider criteria points 11.1 – 11.6.

What do you need to do?
Adults who care for children should have a good understanding of children's development, gained through training or experience. Training and support will be necessary for the staff in managing a wide range of behaviour, and your local support worker should be able to advise you on what is available in your area.

Staff also need to be aware of your policy and procedures on behaviour, if a consistent approach is to be maintained. New and existing staff should either have their own copies of the documents, or have access to them for reference. Parents will need to be aware, through your policy statement, of how children's behaviour is managed.

The key to good management of children's behaviour lies in your whole approach to different behaviour issues. Consider the following:

- Have the staff read and agreed with the behaviour policy? Were they involved in the discussion when the policy was put together and/or involved in the review?

There are many good books available on child development. For example:

A Practical Guide to Child Development
Christine Hobart and Jill Frankel
(Stanley Thornes
ISBN 0-7487-1742-0).

Babies and Young Children, Book 1 Early Years Development Beaver, Brewster, Jones, Keene, Neaum, Tallack
(Stanley Thornes
ISBN 0-7487-3974-2).

From Birth to Five Years
Mary Sheridan (Routledge
ISBN 0-4151-6458-3).

- Do staff praise children's efforts? Building children's self-esteem is important. You should be aiming to encourage children to become confident – to feel good about themselves.

- Do you let children learn by their mistakes? They should be encouraged to experiment, have a go, and discover why something did not work out. Encourage children to build positive relationships with one another. It is sometimes easy for staff to step in too early if there is a dispute. Children need to learn to negotiate and work out problems, though staff should be prepared to step in if the children react aggressively or unkindly.

- Do staff have the same consistent approach? This is not easy, but staff need to look at ways in which to strike a reasonable balance between too much and too little structure in your setting.

- Do staff focus on encouraging positive behaviour, rather than focusing on what is unacceptable? Sometimes, it is in a child's interest for the staff to ignore certain behaviour, and engage the child in some other activity, rather than making an issue out of what has been observed.

- Are your staff good role models? Children are quick to pick up on adult language and behaviour. How should adults behave? If the staff respect the children, giving them encouragement to try new skills, the children will respect themselves, and develop a sense of achievement in their own abilities. If the staff are positive, and tell the children what strengths they have, the children will become more confident in exploring further, attempting greater challenges and developing the belief that 'I can do this'. Children will attempt new skills without the fear of failure staff show support for their efforts.

- Are the staff firm but fair in their approach to the care of the children, recognising that age and developmental stages need to be considered for each child? You cannot expect the same levels of concentration and understanding among children who are aged between three and five. If you are secure in your knowledge of child development, you will meet the needs of all the children as individuals, and make the appropriate allowances for children when necessary.

- Do staff recognise that all children have needs? These include:
  Love
  Stability
  Sense of belonging
  Security
  Food
  Shelter
  Rest/sleep
  Consistency
  Opportunities to learn/develop
  Companionship

If these needs are met, why do children behave in unacceptable ways at times? Children are human beings, with feelings. They have their own views and opinions on issues. They have likes and dislikes. They may be unwell. They may be tired. They may not understand. There may be factors outside the setting which affect the child's behaviour in the setting, for example, difficulties at home. If there is no consistent routine, a child will not know the boundaries.

All of these points are important if you are to consider each child as an individual, and understand that there may be good reason for a child to behave in a way that may not be acceptable. There must be a way of dealing with unacceptable behaviour, though. How can you address this, keeping the above points in mind?

Firstly, prevention – thinking about what you can do to encourage positive behaviour:

- Working with parents – having clear policies which let parents know what you mean by acceptable behaviour, and what measures you have in place for dealing with unacceptable behaviour.

- Explain the rules to the children – what you expect of them in terms of behaviour, in a way in which they will understand.

- Have books available to help children express their feelings. Books that deal sensitively, for example, with divorce/separation, death, going into hospital, will help the child who has anxieties about such situations.

- Make the most of your home corner, giving children the chance to act out situations and explore their feelings.

- Give children time to talk. It is vital in the early years that children are given the opportunity to tell adults about what is happening in their lives – happy and not so happy times – and for the adult to really listen, taking the messages on board to help the child if necessary.

Any of the above will work if you are considering a preventative approach, but unacceptable behaviour will still be seen at times. Preventative measures are needed, but you also have to be prepared to deal with unacceptable behaviour when it happens.

What about the child who continues to act in an unacceptable way? You must consider the safety aspects for the child, the other children, and the staff, too. If a child is going to cause harm to another person, the word 'no' is likely to be used. This is not a problem, unless you do not follow on with an explanation of why you have said no. Children need explanations – how else will they appreciate why the behaviour was not acceptable? Just saying no is not enough to help a child to understand.

Should you punish children? The dictionary definition of 'punish' is:

'the offender has cause to suffer for his/her offence, inflict a penalty for, treat roughly'. Surely this is not appropriate for childcare settings. You do need to think about the way in which you will deal with the behaviour, but it must be considered from the point of view of the child's age, developmental stage, the situation when the behaviour was shown, and the cause for the behaviour. Rather than punish a child, think about an age appropriate way of dealing with the situation, such as:

- Distraction

- Explanation

- Removing the child from the situation

Certainly, removing the child from the situation – time out, as some settings refer to this – can be effective, but only for a short time, and with an explanation given to the child as to why they have been removed. Raising your voice or speaking unkindly to a child is not effective, in fact, it is more likely to give the child a message that this is the way that they can treat others. Always be respectful to a child, regardless of the way in which the child has behaved, and let the matter drop when you have dealt with it. Children do not need constant reminders of their unacceptable behaviour.

If parents are to be kept informed of their child's development, you would need to advise them of any difficulties, too, either in respect of their general development or behaviour. Parents will need to be advised on any sensitive matter in private. It is not good practice to discuss a child in front of the other children and parents. You and the parents should be working together for the benefit of each child, looking at ways in which to provide a consistent approach to behaviour management.

Dealing with dilemmas

A three-year-old child in your nursery has become aggressive recently and this is out of character. You know the child well and have a good relationship with the parents. The child has attended your setting for more than a year and has been settled until now.

A member of staff in the room where the child is based has become frustrated with the child, as there appears to be no reason for the child's behaviour. Other children have been hit by the child, had toys taken from them, and the child has been generally disruptive. You, as manager, have been informed of this, and have asked the staff to monitor the situation.

As the child seems to be more and more unsettled, you know the time has come to approach the parents about the situation – children are at risk because of the child's unacceptable behaviour.

There is always a reason for the way in which children behave – the cause for unacceptable behaviour has to be found. If the cause cannot be identified through talking with the child, the parents will need to be approached. They would need to be informed at some stage if their child was experiencing problems – it is important to discuss the issues as soon as possible so that the child can be helped.

Have you spoken to the member of staff who has become frustrated with the child? You must do this as they are a key person in helping the child. Showing frustration is not helpful. Staff should be observing the child to see what may be the problem, whilst stepping in to protect other children if necessary.

The observations made by staff will be useful for the parents who may not be noticing such behaviour at home.

When was the behaviour first noticed? Was the child with the same group of children each time? What appeared to be the trigger for the behaviour? What action was taken by the staff responsible for the children in that room? At what point was the manager informed?

The parents need to be asked if they can come in to speak to the manager, and possibly the child's key worker. An open and honest approach is needed - parents would expect this. The manager will need to describe the observed behaviour, and explain how the staff have been dealing with the situation. From this meeting with the parents a strategy needs to be put in place for helping the child.

The parents may be able to shed light on the reasons for the behaviour – it is amazing how many parents do not share information on home matters, as they do not realise that there may be an effect on the child. Equally, there may still be no obvious reason for the child's behaviour. Whatever the outcome of the meeting, the manager should ensure that some plan has been agreed with the parents on how to approach the problem from now on.

It must be made clear to the parents that the purpose of the meeting is to help the child, not for the parents to think that they must discipline the child when they go home. This would not be effective, and would not be fair to the child. The cause must be found with total co-operation between staff and parents.

Keep the parents informed of any developments. Working together will benefit the child.

Good practice

■ Staff should act as good role models.

■ Staff should be able to say no, but follow on with an explanation of why.

■ Staff should not expect perfection. Allow children to make mistakes and learn from one another.

■ Staff could talk to the children about 'How we look after ourselves and each other'. This could form the basis of any behaviour management decisions made for the setting, and the children would have been involved at their level of understanding.

■ Staff are in agreement about the correct way of dealing with unacceptable behaviour – a consistent approach. Parents are fully involved in reaching decisions about their child.

■ If physical restraint is needed, how is this dealt with? A clearly worded agreement with parents should be put together.

■ Staff become more comfortable with managing children's behaviour through training in this area of care.

What will the inspector be looking for?

Records of significant incidents – *written evidence*

Your written statement on behaviour management – *written evidence, and staff following the procedures in place – showing a consistent approach*

A named member of staff with responsibility for behaviour management issues – *it may be that you have a designated person in your setting responsible for this area of care*

The standard to be reached:
Adults caring for children in the provision are able to manage a wide range of children's behaviour in a way which promotes their welfare and development.

Most settings have an agreed policy and procedure for all staff, which is reviewed regularly at, for example, a staff meeting. How you approach this area of care is individual to your setting. Your local support worker can help with the wording of your policy in respect of behaviour management. A named person in your setting may be responsible for contacting someone for advice, but it is usually the manager or supervisor.

Childminders who are caring for children in their own home may also be caring for their own children at the same time. Approaches to managing children's behaviour will need careful consideration, as the age range of children may vary from babies to eight-year-olds and over. You need to consider criteria points 11.1 – 11.7.

Through your discussion and written contract with parents, you will have agreed a number of things, including management of the child's behaviour. Your registration course will have helped with this, and you will also have your own home rules that apply to your own children. Many issues that could arise for you will be similar to those issues for group care (see the section above). The main difference for childminders is that of physical punishments and interventions – criteria points 11.4 – 11.6. In your guidance book, a number of points have been listed for you to consider. It has been made clear that, with written agreement from the parents, you may smack their child. But consider the following points:

What do you do if one set of parents asks you to smack their child if you feel the child's behaviour is unacceptable, but another set of parents asks you not to? Could you comfortably smack a child in front of another child, and be able to explain why you do not smack both children for the same unacceptable behaviour? Standard 1 considers your suitability to care for children. You will need to demonstrate to the inspector how you will provide consistency of care. You will need to decide whether you are a 'smacking' or 'non-smacking' childminder to demonstrate consistency of care for all the children.

How do you define the word 'smack'? One person may describe a smack on the hand as a tap. Another may say this is a smack. Either way, if you leave a mark on a child, the parent may say 'I know I said you could smack my child, but I did not mean with enough force to leave a mark'. You, as a childminder, may find yourself facing parents who now consider that you have treated their child unkindly.

What is meant by 'naughty'? The Oxford Dictionary defines the word as 'disobedient, behaving badly'. This is not helpful as disobedience or bad behaviour usually has a cause. The child may not understand that the behaviour is unacceptable, the developmental stage of the child will need to be taken into consideration, the child may be ill, or tired. Any number of reasons may affect a child's behaviour, and this is what you should be thinking about.

Look for the cause of the behaviour, and deal with that, and you are likely to find that the child's behaviour will change to be acceptable.

Communicate with the children in your care – find out about what they feel/think about things. A child who has lost a pet, for example, may show their feelings through their behaviour – they may become aggressive or unusually emotional. Surely, you would consider this as an example of a cause for a certain behaviour and respond appropriately. If the child becomes aggressive, and you are aware of the cause, be understanding whilst dealing with the aggression with empathy – understanding the child's situation.

If you are a member of the National Childminding Association (NCMA), you will have agreed to meet their Quality Standards, which include 'Managing children's behaviour'. NCMA childminders:

■ Never smack, shake, bite, frighten or humiliate a child.

■ Take a positive approach to managing children's behaviour.

■ Set clear boundaries for children's behaviour and share these with parents.

■ Give praise and encouragement when children live up to expectations.

■ Respond to unwanted behaviour appropriately, according to the children's age and level of understanding.

The NCMA is keen to ensure that the standards set for childminders are the same as those for carers in group provision. The standards for group settings do not allow children to be smacked.

Working in partnership with parents and carers

The standard to be reached:
The registered person and staff work in partnership with parents to meet the needs of the children, both individually and as a group. Information is shared.

Requirements that you must comply with:
Children Act regulations
You must keep records of the name, address and date of birth of each child and the name, address and telephone number of a parent.

You must keep a statement of the procedure to be followed where a parent has a complaint about your service.

What does this mean for your setting?
If you are to provide a good service to families, you need to focus on more than the care of the children. Your relationship with the parents is important, too. If the staff are confident in their ability to offer quality care, the parents will be happy - secure in the knowledge that your provision is good, with competent staff looking after their children. This will, in turn, have a positive effect on the children, who will see that the relationship between their parents and carers is good. A child will settle where parents and staff work well together.

What do you need to do?
The focus for this standard is on your professional relationship with the parents. How can you achieve this in your setting? You need to consider criteria points 12.1 – 12.8, looking at the following:

- Information for parents
- Volunteers and committee members
- Exchanging information
- Complaints
- Privacy, confidentiality and parental access to records
- Children's departure
- Children in need

Information for parents
Consider your written information. Be prepared to arrange for an interpreter for any family for whom English is not their first language.

How do you make parents aware of your policies and procedures? You are likely to have these documents available, but they will need explaining as well.

Parents will have questions – make time to talk to parents not just when they are new to your setting, but at all times. Think about setting up an appointment system for more formal discussions. In this way, any minor queries can be raised and dealt with before they become major problems.

Sending letters or notices to parents is a good way of making sure that they are kept informed, but remember that not every parent will read – or is able to read - what you send out, so communicate verbally, too. Not every parent will come to you if they have a problem – make it clear that you are always available to speak to them about their child, and make them feel comfortable about approaching you if they need to ask about anything. Sometimes you may sense that a parent has a problem from their expression or body language. If you think that they are worried about something you should ask them if everything is okay. The parent then has the chance to say something. Sometimes, information on a noticeboard will answer parents' questions – the noticeboard should be a focal point of any setting.

The key to working well with parents is sharing information. You should take the lead in this, with an open approach to dealing with parents, and inviting comment from parents on all issues that affect the setting. You will then be really working in partnership.

Volunteers and committee members
Not all settings have volunteers and/or committee members. For those that do, clear guidance should be in place for their involvement. For example, you need to have clear descriptions of their responsibilities. They should not be left unsupervised with the children at any time until full references have been taken up. Induction is important for all new staff, and anyone else that will be spending time in your setting. For volunteers and committee members, who may not know, for example, the layout of the building, where resources are kept, and where cleaning materials are stored, induction would provide them with the information they need. Are all staff and volunteers easily identified by parents? Name badges are useful where no uniform is worn.

Exchanging information
This should always be a two-way process. You need information about the children, and parents need

information from you about your setting, and how you will be meeting their child's needs. It is important that you have the details of each child on a register, with the date of birth, address and any medical needs recorded. Keep all of this information in one place. If you need to evacuate the building, you will have all the information you need to contact parents. You should also keep a record of the staff working on each day, with an emergency contact for each one, in case of any medical emergency. This information can be kept in the back of the main register.

Parents need to be kept informed regularly about what is going on. If you operate a key worker system, this person will be the main point of contact for parents. He or she should make sure that all information is shared with the parents verbally.

Some settings have a comment or suggestion box for parents, others use termly newsletters to ask for views. If you organise open days/mornings, involve parents in the arrangements – all of these things will strengthen your relationships with them, whilst at the same time ensuring that information is exchanged. Remember, too, that children's needs change as they develop – you will need to have a continuous exchange of information with parents about meeting the changing needs of the children.

Complaints

At some time you may have to deal with a parent who is not happy about an aspect of care provided by your setting. It may be that there has been a misunderstanding, resulting in the parent feeling that something is wrong. How can these situations be avoided? The answer is within your communication process.

What do we mean by 'complaint'? It may be that the parent has a concern or general enquiry that can be addressed easily by the staff. However, if a parent has more serious concerns about quality of care, an inappropriate response to a child, health and safety issues or allegations of abuse, this would need some form of investigation. (Allegations of abuse are considered under Standard 13, Child protection, see pages 56-59.)

It is your responsibility to advise parents on what course of action is available to them if they have a serious concern that would be described as a complaint against the setting. You should have a complaint procedure for your setting. Parents should know that you are always available to discuss any concerns they may have. If a parent is unable to resolve an issue with you, or feels that they are unable to raise the issue as it is so serious, you must give them the contact details for Ofsted Early Years Directorate (Investigation and complaint team). This information should be available to all parents.

Clearly, any complaint made against a setting will be upsetting for all those involved. You will need always to make sure that all your records - assessments, accident and incident reports - are up-to-date. Insurance must be valid – you should have the certificate available. It is important that any complaints are dealt with quickly. Let parents know that you will respond to any concern they may raise with you, but if the complaint needs to be raised with Ofsted, the time scale for any investigation will be organised through them. Of course, you would hope to resolve any situation directly with the parents, and this should be made clear in your written information to parents.

Privacy, confidentiality and parental access to records

Think about where and when you speak to parents. Generally, you welcome parents into your setting and speak to them in front of other people. There may be a time when you need to speak to a parent on a private matter. A separate room or area is needed for this. Confidentiality is important.

Where do you store records on the children, staff and volunteers? Only those people who need access to information should have access. Parents should be aware of any records you keep on their child, be advised on the purpose of the records, and be allowed access to the records.

Dealing with dilemmas

You are a registered childminder caring for two children (aged two and four) as well as your own child, who will be four in a month's time. You have planned to hold a birthday party, with a number of children due to attend. Both of your minded children are due to be cared for on the day, and they are also invited to the party. Your dilemma is that the four-year-old minded child is a Jehovah's Witness, and the family do not celebrate birthdays. How will you deal with this?

You will have been aware from the start of this arrangement that the family are Jehovah's Witnesses, and this would have been the time to discuss any problems that may arise, such as birthday celebrations for your own or other minded children, or Christmas celebrations. You have two main options to offer the parent:

1. That their child is welcome to join in with the birthday party. It may be that the views of the parents are not strict.

2. That they may choose not to bring their child on that day. Other arrangements could be made by the parents themselves, or perhaps you know of other registered childminders in your area that could help for one day. This would only work if the childminder had a vacancy, and also if the child would not be upset by a change of carer for one day. Remember, the child's views matter, too.

It is not for anyone to judge a family on their religious beliefs, whether it affects routine, diet or any other issue that may be different to the views of your own family.

The answer is to discuss the issues with the parents and work out how the child can be accommodated. An open discussion when you first meet the parents is the key to a successful arrangement for the care of any child.

of these children, in respect of the liaison you will need to have with outside agencies as well as with the parents. If a child is placed in your setting through the local authority, you will be given support and advice on how best to help the family. Your local support worker can advise you in these situations.

Good practice

- Consider all you do in respect of care of children from the parent's point of view.
- Do your written statements make sense to a parent who has never placed a child in a day care setting before?
- How welcoming are the staff to all families? Is there a real understanding of the importance of discussing each child's needs? Could this be a training issue for some of your staff?
- Do you promote your setting in the local community, and invite people in to talk to the children? Do you ask parents to come in to talk to the children, or help on a regular basis?
- Is your setting family friendly? Do you display the children's work with pride, and display posters that reflect the society in which we live?

What will the inspector be looking for?

The information you give to parents about the setting, including policies and procedures – *written evidence*

Written agreements with the parents – *contracts or booking forms*

Records of parent's details – *written evidence*

Children's records – *written evidence, registers*

Your complaint procedure – *written evidence, and any parent concerns raised verbally*

Children's departure

You must have a system in place for marking children's names off the register when they leave your premises. This is important, as you need to be aware of who is on the premises at all times, in case of evacuation. If a parent is unable to collect their child, an emergency person can collect, but this should be a clear agreement between you and the parents. The named person should supply you with a photograph, to be attached to the child's detail form, so that identification is no problem.

You also need to think about the situation that may arise if neither of the parents or emergency contact person arrives to collect the child.

How long do you wait before you call social services for help? You would need to contact your local social services department after about half an hour, if you were still not able to make contact with parents or other contact. Social services are in a position to help find relatives who could take the child until the parents have been contacted.

It is fairly common for parents not to keep settings updated on changes to phone numbers. It is in everyone's best interests to send out regular reminders for updated information.

Children in need

Children may be placed in your setting who are in need, due to a number of reasons. You should pay particular regard to the circumstances

The standard to be reached:
The registered person and staff work in partnership with parents to meet the needs of the children, both individually and as a group. Information is shared.

Requirement that you must comply with: Children Act regulations
You must keep records of the name, address and date of birth of each child and the name, address and telephone number of a parent.

■ Transport for outings

■ Behaviour

■ Television

■ Food and drink

There are more examples in your guidance book. Think about the contract you have with the parents – do you review it often to reflect the changing needs of the child? Do you inform parents regularly on matters relating to their child's overall development?

Most childminders exchange information with parents informally, on a verbal basis. This usually works well, although more and more childminders are starting to use written daily diaries as well. This is appreciated by many parents, who like to read about what their child has been doing at the childminder's home.

Certain forms or documents are advisable for the professional image of

the childminder, such as development check forms and activity plans, but some are required under the Children Act regulations. You will need to be able to produce register details of all the children in your care, with contact details of the parents.

If you were the parent, you would probably like to have certain agreements with the person who is to care for your child about, for example:

Your relationship with parents is worth developing if you are to consider the importance to the child of you getting on well with his or her parents. A settled child is a happy child. But there may be occasions when a parent is dissatisfied with you for some reason, and wishes to complain. When you first meet, and are looking to formalise your arrangements with the parents through a contract, give the parents the details of your regional office for Ofsted Early Years Directorate. Let them know that you are registered under the Children Act 1989 by Ofsted, or with the local authority if your transitional inspection has not taken place. If the parents have any concerns, they will hopefully speak to you directly. However, they do need to be aware of who they can contact otherwise.

Child protection

The standard to be reached:
The registered person complies with local child protection procedures approved by the Area Child Protection Committee and ensures that all adults working and looking after children in the provision are able to put the procedures into practice.

Requirement that you must comply with: Children Act regulations
You must keep a statement of the arrangements in place for the protection of each child, including arrangements to safeguard children from abuse or neglect and the procedures to be followed in the event of allegations of abuse or neglect.

What does this mean for your setting?

It is easy to say that the welfare, safety and protection of all children is of paramount importance, but how do you achieve this? If we think about children being vulnerable and in need of adult protection, we have a starting point. Children do not always recognise dangers, and so it is the adult's responsibility to help them understand when they may be facing a dangerous situation, and guide them towards thinking of their own safety.

This seems simple enough if we are considering, for example, water safety, or using a climbing frame. Children will come to understand that they may get injured in certain situations, and that they need to think about what they are doing to make sure that they can play safely.

But your primary consideration is not just the safety of children as they play but their whole well-being. This means that you need to be aware of child protection issues. The information under this standard is not enough for your staff – training in this sensitive area is necessary for all of your staff, so that they understand fully their responsibilities to the children in their care.

What do you need to do?

The standard is clear. Criteria point 13.1 says: 'Coping with concerns about the possible abuse of a child is very stressful for all involved, however your first responsibility is to the child. This means that every member of staff, volunteer or student needs to know about signs of abuse and what to do if concerns arise about possible abuse or neglect'. You need to consider criteria points 13.1 – 13.4.

Written statement

You are not alone in producing a written statement about child protection in your setting. There is help available. You should have a copy of your Area Child Protection Committee procedures – this is your starting point. The information is not just for day care provision, but for all people who work in any capacity with children, including schools. The book will explain in detail about the law, and how this affects you in your work with young children. It explains what the term abuse means. It is also clear that you have a duty to protect the children in your care from abuse.

How can you word this sensitively in your policy and procedure documents, so that parents fully appreciate that you are acting at all times in the best interests of the children? You could consider approaching the issues in the following way:

'The safety and well-being of your child is our primary responsibility. If we have any concerns about your child, we will speak to you in the first instance, and hope that you will approach your key worker if you have any concerns about your child.'
This statement tells parents that nothing matters more than the welfare of their child, and that you would not hesitate to speak to them about any concerns you may have. This should be a reassurance.

'Our staff have attended training in child protection issues, and understand their responsibilities in safeguarding children.'
This statement tells parents that the staff have the knowledge necessary to address any issues relating to the welfare of children. This, too, should be a reassurance to parents, who will appreciate you being alert to these matters.

'We follow the procedures set out in the Area Child Protection Committee procedure book. It is our duty to report any concern we may have regarding the children in our care. This is primarily to safeguard the children.'
Parents will be clear about your role in safeguarding their children.

'We have a designated member of staff who is our liaison person for child protection. This person is able to contact the local child protection co-ordinator within social services for advice on child protection matters. If a member of staff has a concern about a child, the designated member of staff will be informed. A decision about how to inform you of our concerns will be made with minimum people involved. We work within the bounds of confidentiality.'

Parents will be clear that you have a duty to protect children, and would contact the child protection co-ordinator for advice if necessary.

Your main concern is for the welfare of the children in your setting. The staff should all be aware of their responsibility in this area, but should also be aware of the importance of protecting themselves against allegations of abuse. In a group setting, it is unlikely that a member of staff would be alone for more than a couple of minutes with a child, but this may happen if, for example, a child had an accident, and needed to be taken to the toilet area to be changed. The member of staff could protect themselves by:

Telling other staff that the child is about to be taken to the toilet area to be changed. Staying in sight of other adults, if possible.

Dealing as quickly as possible with the child, and then returning to the main group.

Telling another member of staff what they have done, and then advising the parent of the situation when the child is collected.

In this way, they have cared appropriately for the child, made sure that someone knows what they were doing, and then advised the parents at the end of the day/session.

Staff roles
A designated person should be appointed to be responsible for liaison with local child protection agencies. This will not be an easy role, and it is likely that training will be required. Appropriate support will be needed for this person at times. The designated member of staff will need to have good working relationships with all staff, as they will be the person to whom concerned staff will need to speak. The responsibility of the staff is to be aware of each child, and be able to recognise when there is a problem. If a child gives cause for concern, the member of staff will

need to tell the appropriate person, who may be the group SENCO, manager/supervisor, or the child protection designated person. The course of action can then be discussed.

Good practice
■ In some settings, children attend for long hours. It may be that the staff are the first to notice that something is wrong. Your policy and procedure documents must be clear for the staff to use, and for parents to understand. Staff must know what to do if abuse is suspected or disclosed.

■ Children's records should be clear and concise – giving the facts.

■ Staff must be knowledgeable about child development, so that early

Dealing with dilemmas

Always be aware of how other people may see your actions – could they be misunderstood? If an allegation of abuse is made against a member of staff, the registered person has a responsibility to take action. Who needs to be informed? The local authority child protection co-ordinator will need to be alerted to the situation, as well as Ofsted Early Years Directorate. An investigation will need to be carried out. This would obviously be difficult for everyone involved, especially the member of staff against whom the allegation was made.

If an allegation of abuse is made, an investigation must take place – the welfare of the child is of paramount importance. Support will be needed for the member of staff before, during and after the investigation. Your local support worker is independent, and would be able to visit to offer such support. When the member of staff is interviewed, it may be agreed that he/she can ask another member of staff to be available for moral support.

The outcome of the investigation will be whether the allegation was proven, and appropriate steps will need to be taken in respect of the position of the member of staff. If the allegation is not proven, the member of staff will obviously need much support from within the setting. The fewer the people that know the situation, the better. Confidentiality must be maintained.

parents in an open way. The documents are there to be discussed. Child abuse is an emotive issue, but parents do need to be aware of the way in which you will protect the children in your care.

What will the inspector be looking for?

Children's records – *written evidence*

Your statement on child protection – *written evidence*

Your procedures for allegations of abuse made against a member of staff or volunteer – *written evidence*

Your arrangements for complying with local procedures – *verbal discussion*

Who your designated member of staff is – *verbal discussion*

signs of difficulties can be identified, and not mistaken for child abuse. The difficulties may be linked to child abuse, and this should be recognised also. The staff should think about the child in a holistic way, not just focusing on one incident. What is happening in the child's life? Are there family factors to consider?

■ There are times when, for example, unexplained bruising or marks appear, that action is needed immediately, whilst the marking is still obvious.

■ Training is necessary for everyone who works with the children in your setting. This is an individual training need, and important for the care of young and vulnerable children.

■ The staff should be aware of the local child protection procedures book.

■ It is important that you share all your policies and procedures with

The standard to be reached:
The registered person complies with local child protection procedures approved by the Area Child Protection Committee and ensures that all adults working with and looking after children in the provision are able to put the procedures into practice.

Requirement that you must comply with:
Children Act regulations
You must notify Ofsted of any allegations of abuse which is alleged to have taken place while the child is in the care of a childminder.

information from the Area Child Protection Committee procedures to follow. Do you know who you need to contact if you are concerned about a child in your care? Would you be able to speak to a parent with confidence about your concerns? Your local support worker and child protection co-ordinator are there for advice and reassurance, or to support you through a situation where abuse has been alleged.

A registered childminder is solely responsible for children in his/her own home. When it comes to child protection, it is vital that the childminder shares all information with parents and has clear, up-to-date records of the children. A friendly but professional relationship is likely to develop between you and the parents – they place a great deal of trust in you as their child's carer. If you are open and honest about any concerns you may have about a child, parents will appreciate your openness. It may be that the parent has concerns, too, but has not been able to raise the issues with you.

You should be aware of your responsibility to children in respect of their welfare. It is likely that you will have talked about child protection on your registration course. One of the main worries for childminders is allegations of abuse against themselves or a member of their family. This worry is not necessary if you put sensible procedures into place regarding the boundaries to care in your home. You are the registered person, responsible for the children at all times. It is not appropriate for other people in your home to take a child to the toilet, change nappies, or be in charge of the children at any time. Any of these situations could lead to an allegation of abuse – you need to ensure that you take full responsibility for the children at all times.

The NCMA's childminding course, the Introduction to Childminding Practice (ICP), has useful guidance for you in respect of allegations:

From time to time, childminders and members of childminder's families are accused of abusing children. The teenage sons of childminders are especially vulnerable to this sort of accusation. Sometimes such an allegation arises because parents are trying to cover up their own abuse of children, and that may be one reason why you should not discuss your suspicions of abuse with parents before sharing your concerns with another professional.

You need to be aware that you are vulnerable to such allegations because you work alone in your own home. One important way of protecting yourself and your family is to keep records of accidents and also of incidents such as a child arriving at your house with signs of an injury, and asking parents to sign your record to show that they accept what has happened or what you have noticed.

If an allegation is made against a childminder or their family, an investigation must be carried out.

This is a difficult issue. Your support worker can offer you advice on ways in which you can protect yourself.

You should have the relevant

Documentation

The standard to be reached:
Records, policies and procedures which are required for the efficient and safe management of the provision and to promote the welfare, care and learning of children, are maintained. Records about individual children are shared with the child's parent.

Requirements that you must comply with: Children Act regulations
Certain records must be kept on the premises and some must be retained for a period of two years.

You must inform Ofsted of any significant changes or events.

This standard links all of the National Standards, as there are written records, policies and procedures necessary for each of the standards listed.

What does this mean for your setting?
Clearly, your organisation and filing systems are important. Where are all your documents and records kept? Who is responsible for keeping the information up to date? How can you be certain that your system for maintaining records is effective? You need to consider criteria points 14.1 – 14.3.

What do you need to do?
Each setting has its own way of writing records and storing them. If the inspector asks about your documentation, you will need to show them where most of it is kept, as it will not be obvious which cupboard, filing cabinet or shelf is used for this purpose. You need to think about the length of time you keep any records, and your guidance book is helpful with this. For example, certain records that relate to individual children must be kept for two years, so you need to think about where they can be safely stored. These records are:

■ Registers

■ Accident records

■ Medication records

They need to be kept because you may, at some time, need to refer back to them for confirmation that a child attended your setting within a certain time and, for example, had an accident whilst in your care. This would be important, as any injury the child sustained whilst in your care may still affect the child after leaving your setting. Your records will show exactly what happened to the child, on what day, at what time and, most importantly, what action was taken.

The importance of dating any records cannot be over emphasised. If you keep folders dated by the month and the year, you will be able to find the information you need at any time. As a general rule, keep all your records for a minimum of two years. Your guidance book states that 'there is no common agreement about the length of time other records should be kept but recent European Court of Human Rights judgements suggest that it could be for as long as 21 years and three months'. This would suggest that your records could be needed as a reference point until each child has reached adulthood.

In reality, many settings will not have previously kept records for many years. However, you will now need to think about the minimum two-year period for storing records. Where can they be kept?

You will need a system that enables you to store past records as well as current ones. Many settings have a filing cabinet which is kept locked for this purpose. If you keep sections of the cabinet for past records – clearly marked – you will have the rest of the cabinet for current records and information.

So, what records and information should you make available? Many settings keep good records of fire practice evacuations, current registers, accident and medication book, insurance details, record of concern forms (child protection), in addition to the welcome leaflet, policies and procedures documents for the whole setting. This is obviously a huge organisational matter. If you work in a pre-school, after school/holiday club, you may not have the facilities to store all your information on site or, for security reasons, you may need to remove all paperwork from the premises each day. Where do you store this confidential material if the premises cannot be used? Your home is the obvious place, but it is important to remember that the records must be locked away, no matter where they are kept. It is your responsibility, as the registered person/people, to ensure that all records are kept securely. Computer records are sometimes kept. You may need to register under the Data Protection Act and advice about this can be sought through your local Citizen's Advice Bureau.

You will be advised of the month when your inspection will take place but not the exact date, so if some of your records are not normally kept on the premises, you will need to be prepared.

Many owners keep the staff details away from the premises. If there has been a disciplinary matter dealt with by the owner, it would be understandable that such records would be kept away from the premises. An inspector would understand about availability of certain records for confidential reasons.

Throughout the year, you need to keep Ofsted informed of what is happening in your setting, with regard to staff changes, alterations to the premises and anything that may affect the day-to-day running of your setting. These points would be regarded as significant changes. It is in your best interests to inform Ofsted in writing of any changes – you will then have a written record that you informed Ofsted and Ofsted will recognise your setting as one that is known for keeping them informed. If a member of your local community were to contact Ofsted about what they believe could be happening to your premises, for example, Ofsted could confirm that they are aware of the situation, and have agreed to your proposals. If you had not informed Ofsted, and just gone ahead with any work, you may expect an unannounced visit from an inspector.

Your guidance book lists the records that must be kept on the premises. This is a Children Act requirement. Under Standard 14, you are advised of the documents/records that the inspector will ask to see for each standard. Use this information to check that you have everything you will need to show the inspector.

How can you achieve this? The registered person/people are responsible for making sure that all policies and procedures are in place. You could make it a policy that all staff and parents are included in how you approach this task. You cannot do it alone – a real team effort is necessary to produce sound and effective policies and procedures that affect the day-to-day work in your setting. If you are to be able to produce these documents for the inspector much work will need to be done, and this cannot be achieved overnight. The important

Dealing with dilemmas

You have managed your setting for several years and believe that you offer a good service to families. You have sound policies and procedures in place, and all staff adhere to them. You carry out regular evacuations for fire practice. Your written records show that the staff are confident in evacuating the premises in a short time.

You plan an evacuation for the middle of the morning. No other staff member is aware that you intend to do this. Your setting is on school premises, and so you always evacuate when the school bell sounds. A whistle is used for your own evacuations.

Just before you blow the whistle, the school bell sounds, and a call from the school office lets you know that this is not a practice – there is a fire in the school. You immediately blow the whistle, and alert senior members of staff to the situation. The children are removed from the building safely.

The school is badly damaged and your setting has some fire damage, including your office. You are asked by the insurers for an inventory of the contents of your building. You kept a full inventory in your office and this has been destroyed. What could have been done about this?

- You do not need to keep duplicate records of all your documents, but it is worth keeping more than one copy of your full inventory on different premises. Your inventory should list everything within your premises, including the office furniture, kitchen equipment, and so on.

- At the time of purchase, you could add the price of each item to your inventory.

- A member of staff could be the designated person for keeping the full inventory up to date. This would mean being responsible for removing items that have been broken/removed from the premises, adding new items and costs to the list, and making sure that new copies are made of the inventory. A copy for the office file, a copy for the treasurer (of a pre-school), a copy for the owner/chairperson could be considered.

- The designated member of staff could update the inventory once a year, liaising with all staff about resources in their work areas.

thing to remember is that policies and procedures are working documents. They need reviewing regularly so that they genuinely reflect what your setting does. These documents form the basis of the operation of your setting. Without them, there is no structure for the staff to build on. This will become obvious to a visiting inspector, so you need to look at how you can produce the policies and procedures for your setting, which will help you in reaching Standard 14.

What is a policy?

This is a document which gives details about what your setting will do. Policies are the agreed course of action for any setting.

What is a procedure?

This is a document which gives details about how the setting will put the policies into action. They are in place for everyone connected to the setting to refer to and follow in respect of child care practice.

What needs to be written in your welcome/information book?

You should give parents general information about your setting. The book/leaflet should tell parents your aims. Parents will want to know about the following before they choose a setting for their child:

- Where you are located

- Opening hours
- Fees
- Who is responsible
- Basic information about what you have to offer in terms of care and education

Where do you start?

Call a meeting of interested people who can work together to produce the documents. Organise the people into small working groups to look at specific policies and procedures. A draft document should be produced for the whole group to agree. There is no point in producing these documents if they are not going to be used. The staff need to implement the documents. A date should be set to review the policies, and this should be

an ongoing process. Your local support worker can help you start this process if you need help in bringing people together initially.

Good practice

- You operate a professional day care setting. How you promote yourself and what the setting has to offer is important, if you want to attract parents. Your documents are a crucial part of this.

- By producing clear and helpful policies and procedures you will be protecting not only the children but yourselves. An induction package for new staff/volunteers/extra help, such as the committee, will be invaluable in ensuring that everyone is working to the same aim – the safety and welfare of each individual child.

- Involving parents in the process of producing policies is good practice. It may be that you and the staff put the policies into draft form first. Parents could be asked for their comments about the draft copy. In this way, you can demonstrate how you work in partnership with parents.

- Set aside a time within the year to

review all your documents systematically. For example, use a staff meeting for the purpose of reviewing the development records you use for the children. Do the staff find them useful? Do they take too much time to complete?

- You could consider setting up a working party to include staff, parents and committee to look over each separate policy and procedure. When any changes have been agreed, the completed document can be signed as an agreement for all staff to work with. There should be access to all policy and procedure documents for the people who work with them.

What will the inspector be looking for?

Information about all the documents you keep – *written evidence*

Where and how long the documents are kept – *locations and verbal discussion*

Whether you have notified Ofsted of changes to your circumstances – *your written communications with Ofsted, and dates when you have contacted Ofsted by phone – who you spoke to and what you were advised to do*

Standard 14
Childminding

The standard to be reached:
Records, policies and procedures which are required for the efficient and safe management of the provision and to promote the welfare, care and learning of children, are maintained. Records about individual children are shared with the child's parent.

Requirements that you must comply with:
Children Act regulations
Certain records must be kept on the premises and some must be retained for a period of two years.
You must notify Ofsted about any significant changes or events.

Records that you must keep on the premises are listed in your guidance book. Confidentiality is an issue. You need to make sure that all paperwork

is kept in a locked cupboard – your own family should not have access to information you hold about the families you work with.

Certain records need to be kept for a minimum of two years – your registers, accident and medication records.

You will be expected to show the inspector your documents. This would not include your business paperwork. You are self employed, and it is your responsibility to manage your finances, and work with the local tax office in respect of your end of year earnings. If you need advice on this, you can contact your support worker or network co-ordinator.

Babies and children under two years

Under the National Standards, 14 areas need to be considered by each setting, but there are additional criteria to be met by the registered person providing full day care who wishes to care for babies.

You need to think about Standard 2 – Organisation. You need to consider the suitability of the person who will be caring for the under twos:
- their qualifications
- their experience
- their understanding of meeting the needs of the very young in a setting such as yours.

You need to think about Standard 3 – Care, learning and play. Babies need much of your time and attention because they rely on you to meet their needs. You cannot really plan for this, as each day will be different with this age group. Your routine can be planned, but this will need flexibility as the babies' needs come first. You can provide a range of play equipment, but this does not compensate for the direct involvement you should have with the babies and children under two. Physical contact is necessary – babies and children need love and attention, your attention. Sit on the floor with them, join in with their play, as well as letting them explore for themselves.

It is important that you employ a person with relevant qualifications and experience for this age group. Can they demonstrate how they would meet the needs of all the babies, provide play materials to enable the babies to develop, and have a flexible routine that links with routines from home?

You need to think about Standard 4 - Physical environment. Babies and children under the age of two years can be accommodated in one room/area, but this takes some planning if you are to meet the care needs of the children. Is the nappy change area within the room? Would ratios be affected if one member of staff had to go to another area to change one baby's nappy? Is there a separate sleep area to allow the young children the rest they need? Do you partition off a section of the room to allow smaller babies the opportunity to crawl, whilst the older babies become more mobile on their feet? Do staff have comfortable chairs on which to sit to feed the babies? Are chairs available for parents who wish to discuss their babies' needs, such as weaning?

Think about the baby's longer term development, too. Are there opportunities for the babies to spend time with the older children in your setting? Can siblings spend time together during the day? Consider in your own setting how you could allow all the children to mix and play together. This is good practice, as it helps all age groups to have some understanding of each other, and does not restrict children to their own rooms/areas. Think of this as a family type setting – children of all ages together at times.

You need to think about Standard 5 – Equipment. Resources can be shared throughout your setting, however, there will need to be some restrictions for the babies. Age appropriate toys and equipment will need to be considered separately for the under twos, mainly for safety reasons. Providing a wide range of play materials on the floor seems obvious. However, it is surprising how many settings 'display' toys, in an effort to make the room appealing to parents rather than to the babies! Staff should be aware of cleanliness in the area where the babies are cared for.

You need to think about Standard 6 – Safety. Routine is the important factor in a baby room. Staff need to follow set routines for checking sleeping babies, cleaning, making up feeds and strapping children into prams/pushchairs and highchairs. Staff need to be individually responsible for these things – never leave safety issues to someone else.

You need to think about Standard 8 – Food and drink. Staff caring for the under twos have a responsibility to help children make the transition from being bottle fed to independent eating, but this should be in partnership with the parents. When should babies be weaned? At what age should a baby not be given a bottle? When should cutlery be introduced? What food should be given to each baby? The answer to these questions lies with parents – they are the primary carers. You may be asked for advice on these matters, particularly from new parents, but this is advice only – you should take your lead from the parents. If a separate milk kitchen is to be used to prepare the feeds, staff should have a good understanding of the processes needed to prepare feeds and be clear about hygiene matters.

You need to think about Standard 12 – Partnership with parents. Verbal exchanges of information are necessary with the parents of the under twos, although many settings have a daily record sheet, too. As babies develop, their needs change, and staff should be working closely with the parents to ensure that changing needs are met. This will mean time being found to talk to the parents. An appointment system is best for this, as you may find that you will be neglecting other babies as you speak for a length of time to one parent. If cover can be arranged with other staff, you may be able to offer a flexible 'talk' time with parents.

Overnight care

There are additional criteria to be met by a registered person providing full day care who wishes to care for children overnight. There are additional criteria to be met by childminders who wish to care for children overnight. If a child is cared for for a continuous period of 28 days or more, he/she is regarded as a foster child and the carer must notify their local social services department.

There are obvious additional care needs for children who are being cared for overnight.

You need to think about Standard 2 – Organisation. Any person left in charge overnight needs to meet the requirements for supervisory staff. A childminder who works alone will be the person 'in charge' as the overnight care is taking place in the childminder's home. Insurance needs to be considered to be certain that overnight care is comprehensively covered. Childminders need to consider the rest of the household – do you have a separate room for the minded child? The child must have their own bed with fresh bed linen. Has every person in your home over the age of 16 years undergone a police check? In group care, overnight responsibilities may be shared by a number of staff – your procedures should be clear about each staff member's role.

You need to think about Standard 4 – Physical environment. The child being cared for overnight may not have been cared for away from home before – it is your responsibility to make sure that the child feels comfortable. Ask the child if everything is okay. Recognise that the child may be not familiar with your environment in terms of sleeping. Where the child sleeps in relation to others on the premises needs careful

thought – you need to think about the protection of staff/yourself in this area of care.

You need to think about Standard 6 – Safety. A full risk assessment will be needed for any premises where children are to be accommodated overnight. You will need to consider evacuation (very different to during the day), security of the building, whether appliances are turned off. Give particular thought to those people who may smoke on your premises – extra care with cigarettes, lighters and matches.

You need to consider Standard 7 – Health. Levels of hygiene must be maintained in the premises. During the day, members of your household may not use the bathroom, but they may do so during the evening – remember that razors, cosmetics, and so on, should be kept out of reach at all times.

You need to consider Standard 8 – Food and drink. Parents will have views on the food and drink their children are offered. During the day, this will have been agreed, but overnight needs should be considered, too. Check if the child has a favourite bedtime drink. Ask the parents if the child usually wakes in the night for a drink. Is the child allowed a supper meal before bedtime? The child will have a settled night if you closely follow their home routine.

You need to consider Standard 12 – Working in partnership with parents and carers. You will need to have a discussion with the parents about the

child's overnight needs. For example, does the child sleep with a light on or take a favourite toy to bed? Does the child sleep with sheets and blankets, or are they used to a duvet? Some parents have strong views on the use of pillows. The child's routine is what matters – follow the routine according to the information given to you by the parent.

You need to consider Standard 14 – Documentation. You are likely to have contact numbers for the parents if you have been caring for their child during the day. The overnight numbers may be different – this will need to be recorded. You may care for a child whose parent will be out of the country, and not contactable. If so, you must ensure that you have a family contact number in case of medical or other emergency. If the child is on any medication, written instructions should be left with you in respect of this.

Remember - the child is your priority. Meet the child's needs, and you will ensure that the child will be settled in your care.

ENGLISH

Gillian Howell
Updated by Madeleine Barnes
Series Editor: **Richard Cooper**

GN01018701

PLEASE NOTE: THIS BOOK MAY NOT BE PHOTOCOPIED OR REPRODUCED AND WE APPRECIATE YOUR HELP IN PROTECTING OUR COPYRIGHT.

Rising Stars UK Ltd, 7 Hatchers Mews, Bermondsey Street, London SE1 3GS

www.risingstars-uk.com

All facts are correct at time of going to press.

First published 2003
Second edition 2008
This edition 2010
Reprinted 2011 (twice), 2012

Text, design and layout © Rising Stars UK Ltd

First edition written by: Gill Matthews, Alison Clarke, Laura Collins and Richard Cooper
Second edition written by: Gillian Howell
Third edition updated by: Madeleine Barnes
Educational consultant: Lorna Pepper
Project management and editorial: Bruce Nicholson
Illustrations: Phill Burrows, Clive Wakfer and Julian Baker
Design: Clive Sutherland
Cover design: Burville-Riley Partnership

Acknowledgements
p50 Photos iStock; p50 Reproduced with kind permission of Go Ape!, www.goape.co.uk; p52 Extract from the video interview with Valerie Bloom recorded for The Poetry Archive website at www.poetryarchive.org, reprinted by permission of Valerie Bloom and the Poetry Archive; p52 Reproduced with kind permission from *Bootleg* by Alex Shearer (Macmillan Children's Books, London, UK, 2003); p56 Reproduced with kind permission of The Society of Authors as the Literary Representative of the Estate of Alfred Noyes

Every effort has been made to trace copyright holders and obtain their permission for the use of copyright material. The authors and publishers will gladly receive information enabling them to rectify any error or omission in subsequent editions.

All rights reserved. No part of this publication may be reproduced, stored in a retrieval system, or transmitted in any form by any means, electronic, mechanical, photocopying, recording or otherwise, without the prior permission of Rising Stars UK Ltd.

British Library Cataloguing in Publication Data
A CIP record for this book is available from the British Library.

ISBN 978-1-84680-773-2

Printed by Craft Print International Ltd, Singapore

Contents

How to use this book

Writing non-fiction

(1) **Definition** – This describes the genre and provides examples of the text type.

(2) **Text type** – Each type of writing is explained in a step-by-step way to help you plan.

(3) **Self-assessment** – Tick the face that best describes your understanding of this concept.

(4) **Text plan** – Planning is very important when writing fiction and non-fiction, and these charts will help you to plan properly. You are given planning time in the tests, so make sure you use it!

(5) **Language features** – This explains the language features used for this type of text, including examples.

(6) **Text example** – This gives you an example of a well-written piece of text that follows the text plan and contains key language features.

(7) **Tips** – Here you are given key hints and tips to help you achieve Level 4.

(8) **Challenge** – Here you are asked to find features contained in the text example. The answers can be found on pages 61–63.

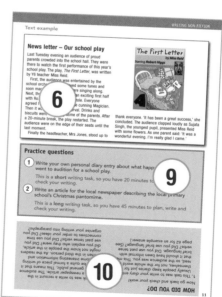

(9) **Practice questions** – This is where you do the work! Try answering the questions by using the text plan and by referring to the key language features. Compare your work with the written example – is it good enough for Level 4?

(10) **How did you do?** – Read the questions – can you answer 'yes' to each of them?

Writing fiction

This section takes you through the key elements of writing fiction:

(1) **Structure** – This section provides a model structure for your fiction writing including examples.

(2) **Setting, character and theme** – This section explains the key ingredients for writing fiction and explores each ingredient in depth.

(3) **Planning** – This section provides you with a structure to use before you begin writing a story.

(4) **Challenge** – The challenges ask you to find features contained in the text example.

(5) **Tips** – The tips give you ideas and hints to improve your work and get the best marks.

Reading comprehension

(1) **Text examples** – These give you typical examples of a piece of text that you might find in your National Tests.

(2) **Tips** – These give you suggestions on how to read the text and questions to ask yourself while reading.

(3) **Questions** – The text is followed by a number of questions relating to the text. There are 1-, 2- and 3-mark questions, so remember to read between the lines.

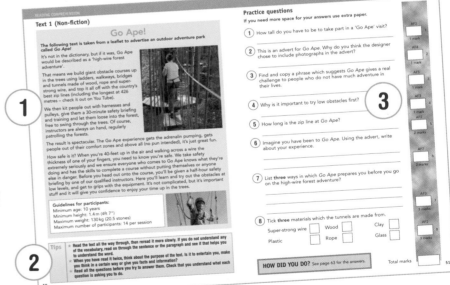

In addition you will find over 100 clear tips and facts to help you with: *grammar   spelling   punctuation   vocabulary   handwriting*

A glossary of terms can be found on page 59.

If you use this guidance to help you prepare for your test you will have a great chance of achieving Level 4!

About the National Tests

Key facts

⭐ The Key Stage 2 National Tests take place in the summer term in Year 6. You will be tested on Maths and English.

⭐ The tests take place in your school and will be marked by examiners – not your teacher!

⭐ Individual scores are not made public. However, a school's combined scores are published in what are commonly known as 'league tables'.

The English National Tests

You will take four tests in English. These are designed to test your reading, writing and spelling. Your handwriting will be assessed through the Longer Writing Task.

The Writing Tasks

There are two Writing Tasks – one shorter and one longer task. Remember to keep your handwriting neat for these tasks.

The *Shorter Writing Task* is 20 minutes long. You should plan very briefly using the given prompts in no longer than two to three minutes. Remember that you only have 20 minutes in total, but still need to include a one-minute check at the end.

The *Longer Writing Task* is 45 minutes long. You should aim for 10 minutes' planning at the most. You must use the given plan and not any other separate paper or planner. However, your planning sheet will not be marked so you do not need to be neat. But remember, you must be able to understand the notes on your plan! Remember ALWAYS to spend three to five minutes at the end for rereading and checking.

The Reading Test

This is one test to assess your reading comprehension. It will last one hour; the first 15 minutes are for reading the texts. In this test you will be given a series of texts and an answer booklet. You use the texts to answer the questions so you need not memorise them. You should refer to the texts closely while you are answering.

The Spelling Test

The spelling test is 10 minutes long. Your test paper will have the text of a passage with some words missing. Your teacher will read the complete passage (or play a CD of someone else reading it). You will then hear the passage a second time, during which you have to write the missing words in the spaces on your test paper.

Test techniques

Before the test

(**1**) When you revise, try revising 'little and often' rather than in long sessions.

(**2**) Read the hints and tips throughout the book to remind you of important points.

(**3**) Revise with a friend. You can encourage and learn from each other.

(**4**) Be prepared – bring your own pens and pencils.

During the test

(**1**) READ THE QUESTION, THEN READ IT AGAIN.

(**2**) If you get stuck, don't linger on the same question – move on! You can come back to it later.

(**3**) Never leave a multiple-choice question. Make an educated guess if you really can't work out the answer.

(**4**) Check to see how many marks a question is worth. Have you 'earned' those marks with your answer?

(**5**) Check your answers after each question. Does your answer look correct?

Where to go to get help

Pages 9, 20, 32 and 49 provide you with a description of what you should aim to do when you are reading and writing at Level 4. You can refer to them at any time to check you are keeping on track to achieve Level 4!

Pages 8–31 are designed to help you succeed in the Writing Test and include information about writing fiction and non-fiction.

Pages 32–43 will help you give 'voice' to your writing, sharpen up your punctuation and improve your grammar.

Pages 44–45 give you practice in spelling, including a list of key words to learn before your test.

Pages 48–57 are designed to help you succeed in the Reading Test and include reading fiction, non-fiction and poetry.

Page 59 contains a glossary to help you understand key terms about writing, reading and grammar.

Pages 61–63 provide the answers to the practice questions.

Writing non-fiction

Achieved?

Non-fiction texts give you information about something or someone.
They also give you facts and, sometimes, opinions.

Type of non-fiction	Definition and purpose	Where you might read an example
Recount	Tells you about something that has already happened. It may include personal opinions and comments	Letters, diaries, newspapers, biographies, autobiographies, magazines
Instructions and procedures	Tell you how to do something in a step-by-step way	Board game instructions, recipes, directions, how to make or repair something
Non-chronological report	Gives you facts about a topic or subject	Encyclopaedias, information books, posters, leaflets, travel guides
Explanation	Tells you how or why something happens or works	Leaflets, posters, manuals, letters, diagrams, information books
Discussion	Gives you information both for and against a topic	Newspaper articles, letters, magazines, information leaflets, posters, speeches
Persuasion	Tries to influence how you think about someone or something	Advertisements, articles, leaflets, spam emails, letters

Tips	★ The tasks in the non-fiction Writing Test do not always tell you what text type you need to write. They often just say '*Write an information text ...*'
	★ So it is important that you:
	• think carefully about the *purpose* and *audience* you are writing for. This will help you know what type of text to write
	• use the correct structure and language features
	• organise your writing into paragraphs
	• use connectives thoughtfully
	• vary the length and type of your sentences
	• try to be adventurous with your choice of words

Achieve Level 4 writing

At Level 4 your writing is lively and thoughtful. You can develop your ideas and organise them according to the purpose of your writing. You can make adventurous choices of vocabulary and use words for effect. You can use complex sentences, and your spelling and punctuation is usually accurate. Your handwriting is fluent, joined and legible.

Over to you!

- Work through each section and don't rush.
- Learn the purpose of the text type.
- Make sure you understand the way it is organised and the key language features.
- Have a go at the challenges and the practice questions.

Tips	The practice questions	
	★ Decide what the *purpose* of the writing is. This is the clue to which text type to write. E.g. *Write a letter describing a weekend away …* Straight away this tells you the text should be a RECOUNT. *Write a letter to persuade someone to …* Straight away this tells you to write a PERSUASIVE text. Get the idea?	★ Decide who the *audience* is. This is the clue to what sort of language to include. E.g. *Write a letter to your best friend …* This tells you to use informal language because you know the audience well. *Write a report for the local museum on …* This tells you to use polite, formal language because you don't know exactly who will be reading it. Get the idea?
	ALWAYS READ THE QUESTION AT LEAST TWICE! Once you have decided on the purpose and audience, plan, write and check your writing.	

Recount

Definition
A recount is a piece of writing that gives information about something that has happened in the past. A recount can include personal feelings and comments.

Purpose
To retell an event or events.

Text plan

1 Introduction   *When* it happened   *Where* it happened   *Who* was involved

2 Events   *What* happened in chronological (time) order

3 Summary   *Why* it happened   *How* someone felt about it

Look at the words in *italics*. You can use these as headings to help you plan a recount.

Think about organising your recount into three paragraphs.

Language features
Events in a recount have already happened, so use verbs in the PAST TENSE, e.g. *We rode to the park* (not *We ride to the park*).

Use TIME CONNECTIVES to link events, e.g. <u>First</u> we played on the swings. <u>Next</u> we fed the ducks. <u>Later</u> we had a picnic.

If you are in the recount, use the FIRST PERSON (*I, we, us*), e.g. <u>We</u> saw seven white ducks.

If you are writing about someone else, use the THIRD PERSON (*he, she, they*), e.g. <u>They</u> went home at 5 o'clock.

Typical style
Recounts can be INFORMAL when you know the audience, e.g. a personal diary or a letter to a friend.

They can be FORMAL when the audience is unknown, e.g. a newspaper article, a biography or an autobiography.

Challenge
Find and list the time connectives in the News letter text example (page 11).

Tip
★ Recounts can be in the form of a letter, diary entry, biography, autobiography, newspaper article, sports report, news report, email or online blog. Remember to think about the purpose of the text.

Text example

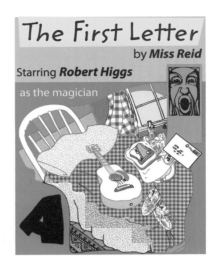

The First Letter
by *Miss Reid*
Starring *Robert Higgs*
as the magician

News letter – Our school play

Last Tuesday evening an audience of proud parents crowded into the school hall. They were there to watch the first performance of this year's school play. The play, *The First Letter*, was written by Y6 teacher Miss Reid.

First, the audience was entertained by the school orchestra. They played some tunes and soon many of the parents were singing along. Next, the play started. It was an exciting first half with Robert Higgs in the lead role. Everyone agreed he was fantastic as the cunning Magician. Then it was time for the interval. Drinks and biscuits were served by some of the parents. After a 20-minute break, the play restarted. The audience were on the edge of their seats until the last moment.

Finally the headteacher, Mrs Jones, stood up to thank everyone. 'It has been a great success,' she concluded. The audience clapped loudly as Sujata Singh, the youngest pupil, presented Miss Reid with some flowers. As one parent said: 'It was a wonderful evening. I'm really glad I came.'

Practice questions

(1) Write your own personal diary entry about what happened when you went to audition for a school play.

This is a **short** writing task, so you have 20 minutes to plan, write and check your writing.

(2) Write an article for the local newspaper describing the local primary school's Christmas pantomime.

This is a **long** writing task, so you have 45 minutes to plan, write and check your writing.

HOW DID YOU DO?

Now go back and check your work!

1. This task was to write your diary entry. Usually people keep diaries just for themselves, not for the whole world to read, so the audience was you. This means that it should have been informal with brief language. Did you use past tense verbs? Did you use brief language? (See page 61 for an example answer.)

2. This task was to write a recount in the form of a newspaper article. The audience was the general public. This means that it should be quite a formal piece of writing with some interesting information and written in the third person. As the readers might not know the people in the article, did you explain who they were? Did you use past tense verbs? Did you use time connectives to order your ideas? Did you organise your writing into paragraphs?

Instructions and procedures

Definition
Instructions tell the reader how to do, make or play something or how to get somewhere.

Purpose
To instruct.

Text plan

1 Aim

> This is the title and tells the reader what the instructions are about.

2 What you need

> A list of the things that are needed to achieve the aim. These are listed in order of use.

3 What you do

> A step-by-stepchronological (time order) sequence of what to do achieve the aim.

So, usually in instructions there is a title and two headings.

You need to decide on the best headings for the instructions you are writing.

A recipe could have *ingredients* and *method* as the headings.

Language features
Use amounts and quantities in the list of things that are needed, e.g.
   3 counters   *1 dice*   *1 pack of cards*

You must write in the PRESENT TENSE. If you start to slip into the past tense, you are writing a recount!

Use commands or the IMPERITAVE VOICE. Put the verb at the beginning of the sentence, e.g. *Cut the paper into a circle*.

Write in the SECOND PERSON. Instructions are talking directly to the reader but you don't need to use the word 'you', e.g. 'Cut the paper.' not '*You cut the paper*.

Use CONNECTIVES that are time related e.g. *first, secondly, finally.*

Sometimes you might need to tell the reader how to carry out the instruction by using adverbs, e.g. *Carefully cut the paper.* The adverb can go before the verb at the beginning of the sentence.

You can use bullet points to help the reader.

Typical style
Use BRIEF LANGUAGE. The reader doesn't want lots of words to wade through if they are following instructions. Be careful not to overload sentences with detail.

Tip ★ Think 'step-by-step'. This will help you to order your writing.

Text example

How to look after a pet dinosaur

What you need

A large garden or open space

Plenty of trees and shrubs

Fresh water

Sturdy container, e.g. bath

Scale polish

Lead

1 Your dinosaur needs plenty of room to roam. Allow him time to explore his new home. Keep an eye on him from a distance.

2 Feed your dinosaur on a regular basis by giving him plenty of fresh leaves and other greenery. Offer several litres of fresh water each day in a container that cannot easily be knocked over.

3 Gently clean the dinosaur with scale polish about twice a week. His skin should look supple.

4 Carefully place a lead around his neck in order to take him out in public. Teach him to follow you and to come when you call.

5 Take care of him and you will have a happy life with your pet dinosaur.

Practice questions

1 You know where there is some buried treasure on a small island in the middle of an ocean. A brave explorer has offered to go and get the treasure for you. Write some instructions that tell him where to find it.

This is a **long** writing task, so you have 45 minutes to plan, write and check your writing.

2 The aliens have landed and want to come to school! Write a set of instructions telling the aliens how to get dressed for school so that they will blend in with the rest of the pupils.

This is a **short** writing task, so you have 20 minutes to plan, write and check your writing.

HOW DID YOU DO?

Now go back and check your work!

1. This task was to write a set of instructions in the form of directions. The audience was a brave explorer looking for some buried treasure. This means that he would need detailed information about how to get to the treasure. You could have told him what landmarks to look out for on the route. Did you think about what he would need to take with him? You could have listed things like a rope and a spade.

2. This task was to write a set of instructions for getting dressed for school. The audience was a group of aliens. They would not be familiar with the names of human clothing nor how to put it on. You would need to describe clothes very carefully and give detailed instructions about how to put the clothes on. But, you only had 20 minutes. You didn't have time to get carried away! (See page 61 for an example answer.)

1.

Non-chronological report

Definition
Non-chronological reports give a reader information about something or somewhere. They are usually about a group of things, e.g. *dinosaurs*, not one thing in particular, e.g. *Dilly the dinosaur*. Facts about the subject are organised into paragraphs.

Purpose
To give information.

Text plan

1 Title — **Usually the subject of the report.**

2 Introduction — **Definition of the subject.**

3 Series of paragraphs about various aspects of the subject — **Facts usually grouped by topic.**

4 Summary or rounding-off statement — **Could be an unusual fact about the subject.**

Paragraphs are the key to writing non-chronological reports. Try to use at least two paragraphs after the introduction and before the rounding-off statement.

Decide what each paragraph is going to be about and only have that information in there.

Language features
Use the PRESENT TENSE if the subject still exists, e.g. *Crocoraffes have, are, live.* Use the PAST TENSE if the subject is from the past, e.g. *Dinosaurs were, had, lived.*

Use TECHNICAL VOCABULARY (language about the subject), e.g. *Many dinosaurs were <u>herbivores</u>.*

Use FACTUAL ADJECTIVES to give more information about a fact, e.g. *They had <u>very sharp</u> teeth and <u>strong</u> jaws.*

Challenge
Write a key word to summarise each of the paragraphs in the text example on page 13.

Typical style
Use IMPERSONAL sentence starts, e.g. sentences that begin with *The crocoraffes ..., They are ..., It is ..., Crocoraffes ...*

Sentences that begin with *I, she, he, we* are personal sentence starts.

Remember always to use IMPERSONAL sentences.

Tip ★ **Reports can be in the form of letters, encyclopaedia entries, information posters or leaflets, as well as straightforward pieces of writing.**

Text example

Crocoraffes

Crocoraffes are large animals. They can breathe and eat, both in and out of water. They were discovered on 1 April 2008 by the explorer Sir Humbert Bumbert while he was trekking through dense jungle.

Crocoraffes are about the size of a large horse and have scaly skin that has a mottled effect. They have long necks, which they use to reach up into the highest branches for leaves. They also have very sharp teeth and strong jaws in order to catch their prey when swimming under water. The animal's broad muscular legs push it quickly through water.

Crocoraffes are omnivores. This means that they eat both leaves and meat. They are attracted by the tender new shoots of the honey tree and can cause considerable damage to these trees. In the water, crocoraffes will catch and eat up to fifty large fish in a day.

The jungles of South America appear to be the only place where crocoraffes can be found. They keep to the thickest part of the jungle that is rarely, if ever, visited by people. They make large nests from jungle creepers and line them with mud from the river bank. This hardens to create a sturdy home for a pair of crocoraffes and their offspring.

They can live for as long as forty to fifty years and mate for life. During this partnership a couple can produce as many as a hundred offspring, known as crocoraffettes.

Practice questions

1. Your task is to write a leaflet to display outside the main enclosure of Sir Humbert Bumbert's Butterfly Farm that houses all the rare and unusual butterfly species he has collected on his travels.

   This is a **long** writing task, so you have 45 minutes to plan, write and check your writing.

2. The fossilised skeleton of a newly discovered type of dinosaur has been found. Your task is to write a poster to display in a children's museum to tell visitors about this type of dinosaur.

   This is a **short** writing task, so you have 20 minutes to plan, write and check your writing.

HOW DID YOU DO?

Now go back and check your work!

1. The task was to write a report in the form of a leaflet. The leaflet will be displayed at the Butterfly Farm, so the audience would be the general public. This means that you needed to write in a formal style. In the introduction you should have briefly described what a butterfly farm is and what you can see there. In the next two or three paragraphs you should have chosen different things to write about in more detail, e.g. types of butterfly, habitat, life-cycle. Did you use present tense verbs? You should not have included very much about

2. Your task was to write a report in the form of a poster. This will be displayed at a children's museum so the audience is the general public, but as it is mainly for young people you could have used a slightly informal style. Did you still have the information organised into paragraphs? As this report was in the form of a poster, you should have used brief language. Did you use, for example, bullet points, tables or charts? (See page 61 for an example answer.)

how and where they were found or it will turn into a recount before your very eyes!

Explanation

Achieved?

Definition
An explanation tells the reader how or why something works or happens. It can be about natural things, e.g. *why volcanoes erupt*, or about mechanical things, e.g. *how a radio works*.

Purpose
To explain.

Text plan

1 Title

2 Introduction

3 A paragraph describing the parts and/or appearance of the subject or process to be explained

4 A paragraph explaining what something does, or why or how it works, often in time order

5 Concluding paragraph

Tells the reader what the explanation is about. Often contains *how* or *why*.

Tells the reader about the subject or process of the explanation.

Summarising or rounding off. This could include where the subject or process occurs, or its effects.

Language features
Use PRESENT TENSE verbs, e.g. *Ships <u>carry</u> goods.* Use PAST TENSE verbs for historical topics, e.g. *Pirate ships <u>were</u> common.*

Use TIME-BASED CONNECTIVES to show the order in which things happen, e.g. *first, next, finally*.

Use CAUSE AND EFFECT CONNECTIVES to show how one thing makes something else happen, e.g. *as, so that, in order to, because, this results in*.

Use TECHNICAL VOCABULARY (specific language for the subject), e.g. *When the wind blows, the angle of the <u>sails</u> make the ship <u>tack</u>.*

EXPLAIN technical terms if need be. You can define terms in the text, or write a glossary, e.g. *tack: sail into the wind using a zig-zag pattern.*

Typical style
The PASSIVE VOICE, e.g. *Sometimes travellers <u>were captured</u> by pirates*, can make the explanation more formal. Remember to use a variety of sentence types.

Tip	★ Explanations can be in the form of letters, diagrams, information leaflets, encyclopaedia entries and posters.

Text example

How pirates attack! (from *How to be a successful pirate!*)

Pirate ships attack any merchant vessel they think might contain valuable goods or money. If the pirate ship is a well-armed large vessel this does not present a problem, but in reality, pirate ships are not big or well armed.

So how can a small pirate ship overcome a larger vessel that has superior fire-power and a crew that outnumbers them? The main tactics used by pirates should be speed and surprise.

When a ship is seen in the distance, the pirate captain studies it through his telescope and makes an assessment of how far away it is and what booty it contains. He then orders the crew to set the sails to make maximum speed towards the vessel. When the pirates are closer to the target, they slow down and attempt to fool the larger vessel into thinking their ship is harmless. Often they raise the same flag so they appear to come from the same country. Sometimes they even send a distress message using the ship's flags. When the pirates are so close that the other ship cannot escape, they throw off their disguise and raise the Jolly Roger.

Even then, you might think, a ship with a much larger crew and armed with many more cannons would easily be able to resist the attack. Therefore, in order to overcome larger, better armed ships, pirates rely heavily on fear! They swarm onto the deck of the target, shouting and screaming, firing guns with clouds of smoke and creating as much noise and chaos as possible. The famous pirate 'Blackbeard' even has lighted fuses tied in his hair. He looks so fearsome that often crews surrender without putting up any fight at all. All this quick action usually means that the captured crew are defeated.

Next, the Pirate captain offers a deal to the captives: they can join the pirates or be thrown overboard! It is not surprising that many captured seamen become pirates themselves.

Practice questions

(1) You have invented a system to stop pirates from being able to board ships. Shipping companies that have lost their cargo to pirates want to know all about it. Write an article for *Shipping Magazine* explaining how it works.

This is a **long** writing task, so you have 45 minutes to plan, write and check your writing.

(2) Your class has invented a new type of lunch box! Write a letter from your teacher to the parents of your class, explaining how this works.

This is a **short** writing task, so you have 20 minutes to plan, write and check your writing.

HOW DID YOU DO?

Now go back and check your work!

1. This task was to write an explanation in the form of a magazine article. The audience would be the owners of shipping companies, so the article would be formal in style. Did you use paragraphs? Did you use cause and effect language? If you have used past tense verbs, then it has turned into a recount! If you wrote telling the shipping companies how to work the system themselves, then it has turned into instructions!

2. This task was to write an explanation in the form of a letter from your teacher to the parents. (See page 61 for an example answer.)

Discussion

Achieved?
☺ 😐 ☹

Definition
A discussion text or *balanced argument* gives the reader information about an issue from different points of view. Readers are left to make up their own minds about how they feel about the issue.

Purpose
To present opposing points of view about an issue.

Text plan

1 Title — Often in the form of a question.

2 Identifying the issue — Opening paragraph states and explains what the issue is and briefly introduces the main arguments.

3 Points in support of the issue — Arguments for, with supporting evidence.

4 Points opposing the issue — Arguments against, with supporting evidence. You can also use argument/counter-argument, one point at a time.

5 Concluding paragraph — Summarising or rounding off. This sometimes recommends one point of view.

Language features
You can use PRESENT TENSE verbs or the PAST TENSE depending on the issue.

Use LOGICAL CONNECTIVES to organise your argument, e.g. *therefore, consequently, so.*

Use connectives that show the OPPOSITE view, e.g. *on the one hand, on the other hand, but, however, nevertheless.*

Use a CONNECTIVE in the final paragraph to signal that you are SUMMING UP, e.g. *in conclusion, to summarise, finally.*

Use EVIDENCE and EXAMPLES to support the points made. These could be numbers and statistics, facts or quotes.

Typical style
Use an IMPERSONAL STYLE. Say what <u>people</u> think, not what <u>you</u> think. Use the PASSIVE VOICE, e.g. *It is thought that, it is believed.*

Challenge
Find and list the passive verb phrases in the discussion on page 19.

Tip ★ Remember to keep your argument balanced. Write four or five points for, and four or five points against.

Text example

How should pirates be punished?

Everyone agrees that piracy is the greatest problem to our merchant ships this century. Pirates plunder our ships, steal their cargoes, capture our sailors and frequently kill them. Everybody involved in sea-travel seems to have a horror story about pirates.

Recently, there has been a great deal of publicity about what to do to about it. It seems most people think any pirates that are caught should immediately be hanged. People argue that this would act as a warning to others. It would show the young, the poor, beggars and thieves that piracy only leads to one outcome – death. They also argue that pirates don't deserve anything else.

However, there are others who believe that *everyone* has the right to a trial. It is a well-known fact that many seamen have been forced to become pirates when they were themselves captured. The number of unwilling pirates is believed to be as high as 45%. Therefore,

hanging pirates without a trial could mean that many innocent victims would suffer. A spokesperson for PAPT (Pirates Are People Too!) stated recently: 'These pirate-victims would return to an ordinary way of life if given the chance and would become decent citizens.' Consequently, they believe *all* pirates should be given a chance. The ones who decide to give up piracy could also give important information about the others and this could help put an end to piracy altogether.

On the other hand, most people believe such a soft approach would result in more pirates, not fewer.

It has been shown that swift and strong punishment has led to a reduction in petty theft by pick-pockets and others. This may also prove to be the case with piracy.

Whatever the final conclusion, it is clear that this issue is complex and needs detailed discussion by Parliament before a solution can be found.

Practice questions

1. There has been a huge increase in the amount of graffiti on the streets of your town. Some examples of the graffiti are beautifully drawn and coloured, others are just scribble. Your task is to write a TV news report to prompt discussion about what should be done, both to the graffiti artists and to the graffiti itself.

This is a **long** writing task, so you have 45 minutes to plan, write and check your writing.

2. Write a summary using bullet points to help a speaker set the scene for a discussion on 'Should mobile phones be allowed in school?'

This is a **short** writing task, so you have 20 minutes to plan, write and check your writing.

HOW DID YOU DO?

Now go back and check your work!

1. This task was to write a discussion in the form of a TV news report. The audience is the general public, so your writing should be fairly formal. Even though it would be a spoken news report, the issue is important to the audience, so did you organise your points clearly in paragraphs? Did you balance points for and against the issue?

2. This task was to write a discussion in bullet point form to summarise the issue and provide someone with notes about it. Did you identify the issue? Did you write your points briefly, but remember to give some supporting evidence? (See page 61 for an example answer.)

19

Persuasion

Definition
A persuasive text tries to make the reader think, do or buy something.

Purpose
To persuade.

Text plan

1 Identify the main point of the text

Could be a statement or question to grab the reader's attention.

2 Supporting points

Organise the reasons into a paragraph for each point with supporting evidence. Explain how people are being affected by the situation.

3 Summary of key points

Repeat the key points to reinforce them.

4 Call to action

Ask the reader to take some action, e.g. to do something, to buy something, to think something, to go somewhere.

Language features
Normally the PRESENT TENSE is used, but you could move into the past or future depending on the point being made.

Support the reasons with EVIDENCE. This could be numbers and statistics, facts or quotes.

Appeal to your readers' emotions by using EMOTIVE LANGUAGE. Make them think about how what you are saying affects them. Try to make them feel something with words, e.g. *It all costs money and who pays for it? You do!*

Include lots of detail in order to explain your ideas clearly and you will be more persuasive.

Typical style
Use the PASSIVE VOICE if you don't want to say where you are getting your evidence from, e.g. *It is thought ... It is believed ... Studies have shown ...*

Challenge
How many passive verb phrases can you find in the text on page 21? If you can use one or two passive verbs, you will get better marks, but don't overdo it!

Tip

★ Persuasive texts can be in virtually any form. They can be letters, posters, leaflets, newspaper and magazine articles or adverts. Remember to think about the *purpose* of the text. Remember to think about who the *audience* is and which words you choose.

Text example

Dear Mr Jones,

I am writing to complain about the quality of the school dinners on offer recently at St Starvin's Primary School.

There have been no fresh fruit or vegetables offered for the last two weeks. Also the chips and nuggets are always very greasy and unappetising. The standard of desserts is also poor – we have had prunes and semolina every day for a month.

As a result of this a number of Year 6 pupils have refused to eat their lunch and have been tired and unable to concentrate in the afternoons.

It has been proven that five portions of fresh fruit and vegetables should be eaten every day to keep people healthy, particularly children. Studies have also shown that protein eaten at lunch time has the effect of boosting brain-power for the rest of the day. Our National Tests begin in May and many of us are very concerned that our results will suffer as a result of this poor diet! This, of course, would have a very bad effect on the reputation of the school.

Although a small number of pupils enjoy your fried food, the majority of us are keen to maintain a balanced diet and lead a healthy lifestyle.

Could you please provide us with suggestions for alternative menus? A group of us would be happy to help with this as we have many ideas ourselves.

I look forward to hearing from you soon.

Yours sincerely,

Em T. Tum, Class 6D

Practice questions

1 Your class has been told that there won't be any school trips for them this year, due to lack of funds. Write a letter to the school governors to persuade them to hold more fundraising events.

This is a **long** writing task, so you have 45 minutes to plan, write and check your writing.

2 Your school football team is short of players. Write a poster to advertise a try-out session after school.

This is a **short** writing task, so you have 20 minutes to plan, write and check your writing.

HOW DID YOU DO?

Now go back and check your work!

1. This task was to write a persuasive text in the form of a letter. The audience was the school governors. This means that the tone of the letter should be formal. You need to have thought carefully about your point of view and how to appeal to the governors, and supported your point of view with reasons and evidence. Did you organise your letter into paragraphs? Did you reinforce your main point by repetition? Did you ask the governors to take action?

2. This task was to write a persuasive text in the form of a poster. The audience was other children in your school so the tone could be informal. Did you include key information and brief language? Did you remember to attract the readers' attention and use language that appealed to the audience? (See page 61 for an example answer.)

Writing fiction

Fiction texts can be in the form of stories, plays or poetry. The main purpose of fiction is to entertain a reader. It can also make readers think about a theme or an issue, or teach a lesson or moral.

In this section we will concentrate on writing stories.

There are three things that all stories have in common:

Setting   Characters   Theme

Page 23 of this book looks at the way stories are structured.

Page 24 looks at these story 'ingredients'. You need to put all three into the mixture to make a story.

There is a section on each of the ingredients on pages 25–28. Each section provides you with tips, ideas and examples. There are also some practice questions. These are short writing tasks.

Stories need planning! On pages 30 and 31 you will find ideas to help you plan. Planning is important, so don't skip this bit!

Over to you!
- Work through each section carefully.
- Make sure you understand what you want your reader to think or feel.
- Have a go at the practice questions.
- Look back at the section. Have you included the right sort of detail in the right sort of way?

Achieve Level 4 Writing
At Level 4 your writing is lively and thoughtful. You can develop your ideas and organise them according to the purpose of your writing. You can make adventurous choices of vocabulary and use words for effect. You can use a variety of sentence types including complex sentences, and your spelling and punctuation is usually accurate. Your handwriting is fluent, joined and legible.

Tips	★ All writers 'borrow' ideas from other writers, so read as much as you can! Note down ideas, sentences, phrases and words that you like. Use them in your own writing.
	★ Keep a 'writing ideas' book.
	★ Your reader doesn't know what is happening inside your head while you write, so make sure you tell or show them.
	★ When your characters are talking, tell the reader who is speaking.
	★ Use paragraphs. Think *Person, Time, Place* (PTP). When the person, time or place changes in your story, start a new paragraph.

Story structure

Achieved?
☺ 😐 ☹

All stories are organised in the same basic way.

When you plan your story, think in five sections:

1 Beginning — **Introduce the setting and the main characters.**

2 Build-up — **The story gets going. The characters start to do something.**

3 Problem — **Something goes wrong! This is the most exciting part of the story.**

4 Resolution — **The problem gets sorted out.**

5 Ending — **All the loose ends are tied up. The characters think or reflect on what has happened.**

Setting, characters and theme

Achieved?

Before you plan your story, you need to decide on the three main ingredients: setting, characters and theme.

Setting

This is WHEN and WHERE your story takes place. You need to help your readers make a picture in their minds. The setting can also be used to create an atmosphere and affect how the reader feels.

Think about some of the stories you have read. When and where were they set? How do you know? Look at some short stories to see how the authors have told the reader about the setting. Have a go at drawing the setting that you read about.

There is more about story settings on page 25.

Characters

This is WHO is in the story. You need to help the readers build up a picture of the characters – not just APPEARANCE but also PERSONALITY. Your readers need to have an idea of what the characters are like.

Think about the stories you have read. Who were the characters? What were they like? How do you know? What were they called? How did they speak? Look at some short stories to see how authors have told the reader about the characters. Try drawing a character as you see them in your mind's eye.

There is more about character on page 26 and more about dialogue (how characters speak) on page 29.

Theme

This is WHAT happens in the story. Some people say that there are only a few story themes in the world. All writers borrow ideas from other stories and this is something you can do.

Think about stories you have read. What happened? Did one story remind you of any others? List some of the common themes, e.g. good overcomes evil, main character loses something.

There is more about theme on page 28.

Once you have chosen your ingredients, mix them together and make a story!

Setting

Introduce the setting in the beginning section of the story. Remember, the two things you need to tell your readers are *when* and *where* the story is set.

When and where?

The big picture

Is your story set in the past, now or in the future? Look at these three examples. How has the writer told the reader about the big picture?

The spaceship hovered near the planet, waiting for cargo-ships to leave the surface.

Black Jake stuffed his cutlass through his belt, straightened his tricorn hat and began to stride across the quarter deck.

Jon eagerly put his new Harry Potter DVD into the player and pressed Play.

Above, this writer has used objects to tell us when and where the story is set. Spaceships and planets point to the story being set in the future. A cutlass, tri-corn hat and quarter deck tell us this story is probably set in the past. The DVD shows us that the story is set in the present day.

The smaller picture

Writers tell us more about the setting by adding smaller details. Look how the writer tells us about the season when the story takes place.

Twists of dust rose in the heat of the planet's surface as it moved towards the blazing sun.

Black Jake shielded his eyes as the snowflakes grew thicker and peered into the murky distance.

Jon settled down to enjoy the next hour and ignored the rain and wind as they lashed the last of the leaves from the trees outside.

This is a more interesting way than just saying *It was very hot …* or *It was a cold winter day …* or *On a wet autumn afternoon …*

Characters

Introduce your main characters at the beginning of the story. Have a picture of them in your mind. Three things that will make your characters 'real' are:
- what they look like
- what they say and how they say it
- how they move.

What they look like

You can describe the characters' face, hair and clothes.

What do you think the two characters below are like? How has the writer made you feel that way?

> Jack strode to the window, his long black coat flapping around his strong legs. A deep frown creased his forehead and his eyes narrowed dangerously beneath the brim of his hat.

> Her wild tangled hair was only half-tamed by the bits of twine tied into it. Her clothes had seen better days; torn striped breeches and an old lace shirt; but she stood straight and tall as any great lady of society.

Challenge 1

The descriptions above tell us something about the characters' appearance. What else has the writer told us about these characters?

Tip	★ Make sure your descriptions are *important* to your character. Don't waste words when they are not needed in the story!

What they say and how they say it

Dialogue adds interest and variety to your writing. But dialogue needs to move the story along. What has the writer done in these two extracts?

> Jack strode to the window, his long black coat flapping around his strong legs. A deep frown creased his forehead and his eyes narrowed dangerously beneath the brim of his hat. 'Who laughed?' he growled angrily.

> Her wild tangled hair was only half-tamed by the bits of twine tied into it. Her clothes had seen better days; torn striped breeches and an old lace shirt; but she stood straight and tall as any great lady of society. 'Stay where you are!' she cried, her voice trembling.

The writer has added dialogue that tells us what the characters said, but also how they said it by using powerful speech verbs and adverbs.

How they move

Describing how the characters move helps to bring your writing to life. What words has the author used in the extracts above to describe the movement of the characters?

Challenge 2

Write a paragraph describing in your own words how you feel about each of these two characters. Look for *clues* in the descriptions. Think about:

- Appearance – why do they look the way they do?
- Dialogue – what does the dialogue tell you about each character's feelings and personality?
- Movement – what does the way they move tell you about the characters?

Tips	★ **Keep to two or three characters only. If you have two characters, make one male and one female, then there is no confusion about pronouns (*he/she*).** ★ **Only use dialogue when it tells the reader more about the character or the plot. Don't waste words on idle chat.** ★ **Don't tell your reader everything. Give clues!**

Practice questions

1 Old Ben is a very old sailor who is grumpy. His age and experience make him short-tempered with younger sailors. Write a description of how he eats his breakfast on the deck of a busy ship. Remember to give readers clues through action, appearance and dialogue. Give clues – don't tell. Include details about what else is happening around him as he eats, and how he shows his grumpiness and short temper with the younger sailors.

This is a **long** writing task, so you have 45 minutes to plan, write and check your writing.

2 Your best friend is an astronaut. Write a description of her when you meet her as she lands from her latest space mission.

This is a **short** writing task, so you have 20 minutes to plan, write and check your writing. Use the space below to plan your answers.

Theme

Most stories have simple themes:
- Good beats bad
- Lost and found
- Wishing or wanting.

Challenge 1

Which theme do you think belongs to these well-known stories? Discuss your answers with friends or your teacher.

- *The Lord of the Rings*

- *Harry Potter*

- *Cinderella*

Basic structure
Good overcomes evil.

1	Beginning	Two characters – one good, one evil. Setting.
2	Build-up	Evil character plots against good character. Good character is innocently unaware.
3	Problem	Evil character tricks or threatens to harm good character.
4	Resolution	Good character outwits evil character.
5	Ending	Everything is OK. Characters reflect or think about what has happened.

Once you've got the hang of the structure you can start to experiment. You might write a story about a person overcoming a fear or a bully. It's still a similar structure.

Challenge 2

Can you use a grid like this to work out how the themes of **lost and found** and **wishing or wanting** follow the plan?

Now try it with other stories you know.

Dialogue

A story without any dialogue could be very dull. *What* characters say and *how* they say it can tell readers a lot about the characters in a story *and* move the plot along.

Use powerful speech verbs to tell your readers about the character who is speaking.

Consider these examples:
1. *The stranger stood in front of me. 'Move,' he muttered.*
2. *The stranger stood in front of me. 'Move!' he shouted.*
3. *The stranger stood in front of me. 'Move,' he pleaded.*
4. *The stranger stood in front of me. 'Move!' he screamed.*

How do the different speech verbs affect your thoughts:
a) about the character of the stranger?
b) about the plot?

'move...'

'Move!'

'move!'

Challenge

Write a sentence to suggest why 'the stranger' said '*Move*' in each of the four different ways.

'Said' is the speech verb that is used the most but it doesn't tell readers anything about character or plot. Use it when you do not need to add extra detail.

Try to use a variety of powerful and common speech verbs. Don't overuse powerful verbs.

Tips	★ **Dialogue needs to move the story along. Only use it when you want to tell the reader something important about the setting, characters or plot.** ★ **Try to use a variety of verbs *and* adverbs to show how characters are speaking.**

Grammar and punctuation in dialogue
Make it very clear who is speaking. When a new person joins the dialogue, always start their spoken words on a new line.

Use pronouns (*he/she/they*) and the characters' names. See pages 38–39 for further information about punctuation and punctuating dialogue.

Planning

Achieved?

Planning is a very useful way of thinking about story ingredients and organising your ideas. In the KS2 long writing task, you only have about 10 minutes' planning time … not very long at all! So you need to develop a way of planning that is fast and that works for you.

Try using the five-box plan below. Make sure you know the heading for each box and the main things that need to be in that section of the story.

Heading	Main things to include	Example
Beginning	Introduce main character Setting	Joe, boy about 11, into skateboarding. Old empty house, bit spooky.
Build-up	Story gets going	Joe goes into house. Looking for something. Sees paw prints.
Problem	Something goes wrong	Can hear cat but can't get to it. Cat stuck behind wall.
Resolution	Problems sorted out	Joe finds secret button to open wall. Rescues cat.
Ending	Loose ends tied up Characters reflect or think	Everything OK. Joe and cat go off on skateboard.

Now it's just a case of turning your plan into a story. But please remember to refer to your plan while you are writing – don't write something completely different!

1. Practise quickly drawing out the five-box plan and adding the headings. This should take no more than 30 seconds!
2. Now look back at the main things to include. Practise adding the main things to your five boxes. This should take another 30 seconds.
3. Next, practise planning actual stories (you don't need to write them at this stage). Look at some of the long writing tasks on page 31. Read the task carefully, then reread it. Got an idea? Go!
4. Think about the story ingredients you could include. Remember – **setting, characters, theme**. Spend no more than 4 minutes on this. You've now used up 5 minutes of your planning time.
5. Make notes about the ingredients in the boxes. Remember, these are notes, not sentences! You are not writing the story here – you are planning it. Five minutes later – time's up!

> **Tips**
> ★ **Read the task carefully first. Then make notes. Think *setting, characters, theme*. Don't write sentences – you are not writing the story yet, just making a plan. Your plan will not be marked. Then stick to your plan.**
> ★ **A well-planned story will get much better marks than one that rambles and ends abruptly.**

Putting it all together

So, you know the three story ingredients (setting, characters, theme), you know the structure and you know how to plan (five-box plan). It's just a case of putting it all together in a short story.

Remember, in the long writing task you have 10 minutes of planning time and 35 minutes of writing time. This is not very long. You can't afford to have too much detail or make the characters have great adventures. Keep it simple!

Look at the example below. It's about the right length and includes all the story ingredients that you have been reading about.

Tip	★ Make sure you plan the ending for your writing! You will lose marks if you run out of time before showing you can plan the WHOLE story.

The empty house

Joe pushed open the huge wooden door into a large stone-floored hallway. He slipped through the doorway, cobwebs brushing his face. Once inside he breathed in the musty, damp smell of the old empty house.

'Hello!' he called. 'Is anyone there?' All he heard was his own voice echoing around the hall. Looking at the floor he could see paw prints in the dust. He moved forward, tracking them like a hunter in the desert. Then, suddenly, they stopped. Joe found himself staring at a blank wall. There were no more paw prints to be seen.

'Cinders can't have disappeared into thin air,' he muttered. 'Cats don't do that.'

He paused and held his breath. He thought he could hear a faint meowing. He listened hard. His black eyes stood out in his pale face as he knelt down on the floor and put his ear to the wall. Finally his face brightened as he started tapping at the wall.

With a creak, a panel in the wall started to move. The meowing grew louder and Joe's smile grew wider. Eventually the gap in the wall was big enough to reveal … Cinders, Joe's little black cat.

'Oh Cinders, how did you get in there?' asked Joe. Cinders arched her back and purred.

'Come on, let's go,' Joe said. He picked up his skateboard as the pair left the empty house. Placing it on the ground, he patted the front. Cinders jumped on and sat up straight, looking like the proudest cat in town. Joe hopped on behind her and they sped off down the street.

'That's the last time I let you go mouse hunting in there!' Joe told his cat. Cinders blinked and didn't make a sound.

Practice questions

These are **long** writing tasks, so you have 10 minutes to think and plan and 35 minutes to write and check your writing.

1. You are in a big shopping centre with your dad and little sister. Continue the story after this opening sentence, *'Where's little Mari?' asked Dad …*

2. Write a story with this title: 'The mystery of the missing garden gnome'.

3. Write a story that could end with this sentence: *Jamal knew that Butch Brown would never scare him again.'*

4. Write a story with these ingredients: a black cat, an old woman, a scary wood, good overcomes evil.

5. Write a story about a girl who wants to star in the school play.

Grammar

Now you know how to organise your writing for non-fiction and for stories, you know what to include and what to leave out.

Polishing up your grammar could make the final difference to your writing.

In a Level 4 piece of writing, the writer needs to:
- use different types of SENTENCE and PUNCTUATE them correctly
- organise writing into PARAGRAPHS
- use a variety of suitable CONNECTIVES
- choose VOCABULARY carefully.

Tip	★ When you are reading, look carefully at how writers use grammar. Remember, you can 'borrow' their ideas and use them in your own writing.

Remember, to achieve Level 4 you need to use different types of sentence and punctuate them correctly.

- Sentences start with a capital letter and end with a full stop (.), question mark (?) or exclamation mark (!).

- A sentence is made up of one or more clauses.

- There are three main types of sentence – simple, compound and complex. You can use them in different ways to have an effect on your reader.

Three types of sentence

Simple sentences
As the name suggests, simple sentences are easy to write and read. They have one clause: *It was raining.*

Using lots of simple sentences can be very boring for a reader.

I went out. It was raining hard. I put up my brolly. I saw my friend Daisy. I called loudly to her. She came over.

These sentences aren't very interesting for a reader because they are all the same length.

Challenge 1

Can you write your own simple sentence?

Compound sentences

Compound sentences have two or more clauses that are as important as each other. They can be joined by these connectives:

and   but   so

It was raining hard <u>so</u> I put up my brolly.

Tips	★ Be careful that you don't always use *and* to join two clauses.
	★ Learn the connectives in the list so that you can use all of them.

Challenge 2

Can you make your simple sentence into a compound sentence?

Complex sentences

Complex sentences have two or more clauses, but one clause is more important than the others. This is called the *main clause*. A less important clause is called a *subordinate clause*. A subordinate clause is linked to the main clause by a connective:

E.g.   *after   although   as   because   before   if   in case
        once   since   though   unless   until   when   while*

When I left the house, I found it was raining hard so I put up my brolly.

Challenge 3

Try making your compound sentence into a complex sentence.

Mixing sentences

If you always use the same type of sentence, your writing will become boring. You need to use a mix.

Look again at these simple sentences.

I went out. It was raining hard. I put up my brolly. I saw my friend Daisy. I called loudly to her. She came over.

How can they be improved?

I went out. It was raining hard so I put up my brolly. As I was struggling with the catch, I saw my friend Daisy. I called loudly to her. She came over, splashing through the puddles on her way.

Well, that sounds better, doesn't it? Can you spot what's changed? Changing the sentence type means that the reader is given more detail, too.

Using questions

You can have your characters asking questions when they are speaking, but try asking questions in other parts of the story as well.

- *Hanif could just see something through the mist, but what was it?*
- *Why was the table shaking?*
- *How would Jake get out of this fix?*
- *Where were they to go now?*

Asking questions means that the reader asks them too and becomes more interested in the story.

Using exclamations

You can have your characters exclaiming when they speak. You can also use exclamations to make part of a story more interesting.

- *It spoke!*
- *She was stuck!*
- *He jumped!*
- *I was dumbstruck!*

How do they do it?

Let's look at how two children's authors use different sentence types.

The locket

He didn't look back. He set sail into the night, delighted with his daring exploits and laughing with excitement at the thought of the riches he knew would be his. Halfway into his voyage home, he could contain himself no longer and he opened the locket.

The author has used all three sentence types in this extract.

Secrets and eyes

My thirst satisfied, I looked down at the boy in faded Bermuda shorts who had taken my money. He looked at me cautiously with eyes that held the secrets of someone twice his age.

In this extract the author starts a sentence with a subordinate clause.

Challenge 4

Identify a simple sentence, a compound sentence and a complex sentence in the extract 'The locket'.

Practice questions

1. Using *The locket* extract, write a paragraph about the character. Write about where the character had been and what he had done.

2. Describe the contents of the locket and the character's reaction to it using a compound sentence. Use a simple sentence to keep the reader in suspense.

Challenge 5

Continue the story *Secrets and eyes* using a variety of types and lengths of sentence.

Tips	★ Look at books in your classroom and find examples of how authors use different sentence types in their writing.
	★ Try using some of their sentences as models for your own writing.

35

Types of connectives

Achieved?

Remember, when you write you should use a variety of suitable connectives.

Connectives are words and phrases that link ideas (clauses) and sentences or introduce new paragraphs.

If you look back at the non-fiction section on pages 8–21, the types of connective that you can use for different text types are listed.

> There are different connectives for different purposes.

You need to know what a connective means before you can use it. It is very tempting to impress a marker with higher-level connectives, but this can happen:

Hope put her coat *and* her scarf on. *Furthermore* she put on her boots. *Meanwhile* her friends came round. *On the other hand* they went to the park.

Although the above paragraph uses Level 4 connectives, it is not fluent and the connectives do not make sense.

Challenge

Rewrite the above paragraph using connectives that make sense.

Tip	★ When you are reading, make a note of the connectives the author has used. Think about how they have moved the story along.

Try to remember connectives in these groups:

Instead of using 'and' – to add extra information	**To show time passing –** instructions, story writing	
• also • as well as • moreover • too	• next • first, second, third… • meanwhile • after	• then • finally • eventually • before

To emphasise or stress your point – arguments, discussion		**Comparing connectives –** to compare ideas, arguments, discussion	
• above all • especially • indeed	• in particular • significantly • notably	• equally • similarly • as with	• in the same way • likewise • like

To explain a point – explanations, arguments, reports		**To show something might happen**	
• because • therefore • consequently	• so • thus	• however • unless • if	• although • except • as long as

To introduce a point – arguments, persuasion		**To contrast and compare –** discussion, arguments	
• for example • for instance • in the case of	• such as • as revealed by	• whereas • alternatively • unlike	• instead of • otherwise • on the other hand

Tips	★ Don't use the same connective over and over again in one piece of writing. ★ Make a list of connectives and learn them. ★ Collect new connectives from your reading.

Challenge

Use these three connectives to make compound sentences from the following simple sentences: a) *because*   b) *although*   c) *until*

1. *The attack began well. They had been warned of our approach.*
2. *The waves continued crashing on the decks. Everything below was soaked through.*
3. *He stopped running. His heart wasn't in it any more.*

Punctuation

Achieved?

Punctuation tells your reader *how* to read your writing.

Without simple punctuation, your writing will be confusing to read and difficult to understand.

Although full stops and capital letters are the first features of punctuation that we learn, they are often the ones we forget.

> Read these words out loud. How does the punctuation change the meaning?
>
> *Now.*   *Now!*   *Now?*   *Now ...*

Whilst trying to use different types of punctuation, we must remember to check and edit what we write, ensuring that full stops and capital letters are used correctly.

Level 4 writers need to use a range of punctuation marks, but it is not a competition to use the most features. Putting brackets, commas, speech marks and question marks into a paragraph will not automatically make it a Level 4 paragraph.

Challenge

Correct the errors in this paragraph.

Mr Walsh was having an awful day. It was windy and wet (so everybody) was inside for lunch time. The children were behaving, like wild animals and the classroom looked like a zoo?

TRICKY PUNCTUATION

Commas

A comma is a punctuation mark that separates part of a sentence.
Use commas to:

1. separate items in a list, e.g.
   Don't forget your football boots, shin pads, water bottle and towel.

2. add extra information, (brackets and dashes can also do this job), e.g.
   Freddie really enjoyed swimming, in the sea, with his Mum and Dad.

3. separate subordinate clauses, e.g.
   In order to pay for her holiday, Claire had to save over a thousand pounds.

SPEECH PUNCTUATION

There are two ways of telling a reader what a character says: indirect speech and direct speech.

Indirect speech

This is also known as 'reported' speech, when you don't use the speakers' exact words but report what they said, e.g.

- *The Captain said that there would be extra rations for the men.*
- *The teacher threatened to give extra homework if their work did not improve.*
- *The doctor told me how she had saved his life.*

Direct speech

You can use the speaker's actual words inside speech marks (' ', or sometimes " ") but there is a bit more punctuation needed!

- The most common punctuation is a comma.
  E.g. *'We are going to have a wonderful time,' he announced.*
  Here the comma is used at the end of the spoken words INSIDE the speech marks.

- If the speaker continues speaking, you need another comma before the next spoken words.
  E.g. *'We are going to have a wonderful time,' he announced, 'and everyone will take part!'*

- If you start the sentence with the speaker and speech verb, the comma comes before the speech mark and the speech begins with a capital letter.
  E.g. *Flora said, 'You don't have to go.'*

- Full stops, exclamation marks and question marks must be placed inside the speech marks.
  E.g. *'I'm not going!' she yelled.*

- And finally – new speaker = new line.
  E.g.*'I'm not going!' she yelled.*
  'Why not?' asked Mr Parker.

Tips	★ Notice that when the speech verb comes in the middle of one continuous sentence, the second group of words inside speech marks do *not* need a capital letter to begin them.
	★ The speech verb or pronoun after the spoken word always begins with a lowercase letter, while a PROPER NOUN begins with a capital, e.g.
	• *'Rubbish,' she said.*
	• *'Rubbish!' answered Mary.*
	• *'Rubbish,' Mary cried.*
	★ If the spoken words end with an exclamation mark or with a question mark, you still use a lowercase letter after the speech mark.

Apostrophes

Achieved?

Take special care with apostrophes! They can change the meaning of a sentence when used badly.

There are only two reasons why you need an apostrophe:
* to show that something belongs to somebody (possession)
* to show that a letter or letters have been missed out (omission).

Possession

The boy's homework shows that the homework belongs to the boy.

Be careful with plural nouns (more than one).
The boy's boots means the boots belonging to one boy.
The boys' boots means the boots belonging to two or more boys.

Omission

Sometimes a letter (or part of a word) is missed out to make a shortened form.

This often occurs in direct speech so that it sounds natural.
Could not becomes *Couldn't*   *Was not* becomes *Wasn't*
Captain can become *Cap'n*

Tips	★ **It** – this is the really tricky one. Learn the rule and you won't make mistakes!
	★ **The apostrophe is ONLY EVER used when a letter is missed out (the shortened form).** E.g. *It is a great adventure* becomes ***It's a great adventure.***
	★ **The apostrophe is NEVER EVER used to show possession with** it.
	★ **NEVER EVER use an apostrophe with plural nouns UNLESS it shows possession.**

Practice question

Read the passage below. All the punctuation has been stolen, even all the capital letters and full stops! Your challenge is to put it back in. Read the passage carefully and out loud before you start and you will see how important punctuation is to readers.

the ship had been becalmed before but never for so long some of the men lay about the decks that baked in the heat others stayed below hoping for cooler air but the smell of so many men in a small space soon sent them on deck again was that a breath of wind asked the first mate hopefully perhaps it was said capn jake i think youre right all hand to the sails he cried his voice reaching all through the tiny ship men women and children went scurrying aloft

Tip
There are:

9 capital letters	7 full stops	5 commas
2 apostrophes	3 sets of speech marks	1 question mark
1 exclamation mark		

Check your answer against the punctuated passage on page 62.

Organisation

Remember, you need to organise your writing into paragraphs.

Once you have carefully planned your writing, you must organise your ideas in a way that helps the reader to follow your writing.

Level 4 writers need to include an opening/introduction, a middle and an ending. Usually the middle consists of TWO paragraphs.

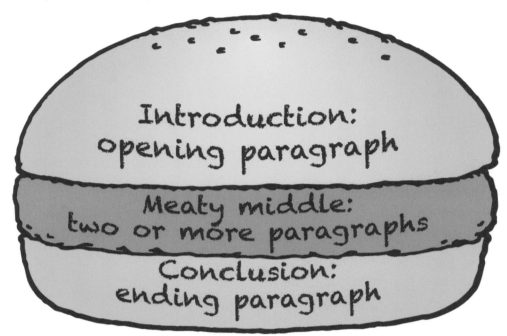

Fiction

Paragraphs usually signal that TIME is passing, or a new PERSON or a place has been introduced. Linking sentences are a good way to open new paragraphs. Here are some ideas:

Soon after
Without warning
This reminded her of the time…

Later on
Just then

Non-fiction

Paragraphs need to link your ideas together in an ARGUMENT, DISCUSSION, RECOUNT, REPORT, EXPLANATION AND LETTER WRITING. Linking sentences used to structure paragraphs in non-fiction could be:

First
Next
This means
As I explained earlier

Then
As a result of
My strongest point is
On the other hand

41

Vocabulary

Think about the words you are going to use in your writing. If you choose them well they can improve the standard of your writing. They can give your reader a clear picture of what you mean and you will get your message across.

Remember, try to avoid repeating favourite words in a single piece of writing.

ADJECTIVES

Adjectives are used to describe a noun. They describe something or someone, e.g.
A red door.
A crying child.

Tips	
★ Avoid using adjectives that say the same thing, e.g. *A frozen icy lake.* Instead, use two adjectives that say something different, e.g. *A vast icy lake.* ★ Avoid using adjectives in writing that you use when chatting, e.g. *really, very, nice, OK.* *We all ate a really nice meal* is dull. *We all ate a delicious meal* is better.	★ Adjectives that have the same initial sound as the noun work well in poetry and fiction. This is called alliteration, e.g. *The magical music.* ★ Remember, only use factual adjectives in non-fiction. Use them to add information, e.g. *The white football* rather than *the gloriously gleaming white football.*

Challenge 1

Change the adjectives in upper case to give readers a better picture in their mind's eye:

1. *This is a GOOD story.*
2. *The train had NICE purple doors.*
3. *After the race his face was VERY RED.*
4. *Mrs Lane is REALLY CROSS.*
5. *The tree had BIG flowers on its branches.*

Adverbs are used to describe a verb. They describe how something is said or done.

- *He gripped tightly.*
- *'I think so,' he answered quietly.*

Adverbs often end in 'ly'.

Challenge 2

Look again at the section on characters on page 26. In the extracts, can you find any adverbs that describe how characters speak or move?

Practice questions 1

Choose an adverb to make these sentences more interesting:

1 *He banged the book onto the table.*

2 *'You look out!' he whispered.*

3 *The monkeys climbed from branch to branch.*

4 *'It wasn't me!' she said.*

VERBS

Verbs tell us what someone or something is doing. Choose your verbs well and it can improve your writing. Which sentence do you think gives a better picture of what is happening?

Sunita put the shoe back into the box.
Sunita slammed the shoe back into the box.

Martin got his hat and raced to the door.
Martin grabbed his hat and raced to the door.

| Tip | ★ Avoid using *put* or *got*. They don't tell the reader much about what is happening. |

Practice questions 2

Choose a new verb to add interest to these sentences:

1 Hordes of menacing monkeys *swung* through the high treetops.

2 The proud princess *walked* along the streets of cheering crowds.

3 She *put* the china cups carefully in the basket.

4 The thief *got* through the broken attic window.

| Tip | ★ In the National Tests you need to show that you can make good vocabulary choices. Have a go at different words. If you get the spelling wrong, you'll still get more marks for choosing good vocabulary than you lose for wrong spelling. |

Spelling

The Spelling Test lasts for 10 minutes. You will be asked to spell 20 words from a passage that your teacher reads to you.

The test will cover:
* basic spelling rules
* more difficult or unusual words that might not fit basic spelling rules.

Below is a list of the 20 most frequently misspelled words in the National Tests over the last few years. Make sure you get them right this year!

change	*nastiest*	*technique*	*stripes*	*advertise*
designed	*swimming*	*perfectly*	*injured*	*regardless*
ready	*future*	*serious*	*attempts*	*vanishing*
produce	*surprise*	*individual*	*known*	*themselves*

The spelling rules that follow will help you. Read them through and make sure you understand them. Then remember to use them when you write.

Plurals

* Most words just add *s*: *road – roads; cup – cups; book – books; cat – cats*

* Some words need *es* to be added. Say them aloud and listen to how they sound. Words that end in a hissing or buzzing sound follow this rule. Words that end in *x, z, ch, sh* and *s* also follow this pattern:
  box – boxes; bus – buses; watch – watches

* Words that end in *f* have a different pattern. You usually need to drop the *f* and add *ves*: *hoof – hooves; wolf – wolves*
  But beware! There are exceptions. Try to learn these words:
  gulf – gulfs; roof – roofs; dwarf – dwarfs/dwarves

* Words that end in *y* have a simple rule. If the letter before *y* is a vowel (*a e i o u*), just add *s*: *way – ways; toy – toys; monkey – monkeys*
  If any other letter (a consonant) comes before the *y*, drop the *y* and add *ies*:
  lady – ladies; spy – spies; story – stories

* Learn the irregular words: *mouse – mice; man – men; child – children.*
  When you are reading, make a note of any irregular plurals you find and learn them.

Challenge

Look through books or dictionaries and find words ending in *y, x, z* and *s*. Change them into plurals.

Practice question

Change these words into plurals:

fox, road, bunch, wish, sound, life, tax, tree, drink, pirate, house, donkey, fly, bus

DOUBLING THE CONSONANT

Adding suffixes -er, -ed or -ing

There is a simple way to understand how to spell words that end in a consonant when you add *-er*, *-ed* or *-ing*. Listen to the sound the vowel makes.

Vowels can make short sounds or long sounds.
Stop has a short 'o' sound.   *Boat* has a long 'o' sound.

The rule is: double the consonant when the vowel is short.
Stop – stopping   *Boat – boating*

Challenge

1. Divide these words into two lists. Put all the words with short vowel sounds in one list, and all the words with the long vowel sounds in the other list.
    bin, line, paper, chat, choose, flutter, reign, wet, meet, light, float, dot

2. Look through some books and add four new words to each list.

3. Add the ending *-er*, *-ed* or *-ing* to the new words to make a different word.

4. Check the vowel sound to see which words need to have a double consonant.

5. Check your spelling in a dictionary.

Quick challenge

Tenses: Put these verbs into the past, present and future tenses. It is a good way to practise many of the spelling rules. If you find spelling some of them hard, look back at the spelling rules and learn them. If you still have trouble getting them right, read as much as you can and practise all you can.

Verb	Past tense	Present tense	Future tense
To fit	I fitted I have fitted I was fitting	I fit I am fitting	I will fit
To move			
To clap			
To keep			
To swim			
To fly			
To produce			
To try			
To pursue			

Reviewing your work

Achieved?
☺ ☹ 😞

Rereading or reviewing your work is an important part of being a writer. No writer thinks their work is finished without rereading it and checking that it makes sense. Don't worry if you find things that need changing – there are always changes to be made. It is a good opportunity to look at ways in which your writing could be improved.

> Here are some ideas to keep in mind when you are reviewing your work.

- **Make sure your reader will understand your main message.** For example, if you are writing a mystery story, will your reader want to find out what happens? Ask yourself if you have given too many clues to the ending. Is there a feeling of suspense and excitement? If you are writing an explanation, have you used connectives to help your reader follow the process that you are explaining? Would you be able to understand the explanation easily? If you are not sure, have another look at the guidelines for writing explanations.

- **Make sure you have followed the guidelines for the text type you are writing.** If you are not sure, go back and check. Keep the style constant and try not to slip from one type of writing to another. If you have started in the first person voice, have you kept to it all the way through your writing? Have you kept to the same verb tense? Don't get worried if you find mistakes – just correct them and try to remember for the future. No one gets it right all the time, but reviewing your work helps you to spot the errors that could lose you marks.

- **Check your spelling and grammar.** Look carefully as you read and, if a word doesn't look right, try it out a few times on a piece of paper. If you can, look it up in a dictionary and try to learn the correct spelling for the future. Read your sentences aloud. This will help you to hear when something doesn't sound right. When you think your grammar is not quite right, try saying the sentence in different ways and rewrite it a few times. Pick the one that you think sounds best and don't be afraid to make changes. Go back and check for any simple mistakes. Have you added all your capital letters and full stops?

Writer's tips	★ **Read as often as you can. Reading helps you become familiar with good writing, helps you remember spelling patterns and helps you learn how to structure your sentences. Read as many kinds of books as you can. This will help you get ideas for your own writing.**
	★ **Keep a notebook and write down ideas, phrases, sentences and words that you like. If you read a phrase that might be useful, don't be afraid to make use of it. You can learn a lot from other writers' ideas. Jot them down in your writer's notebook. You never know when they might come in handy.**

Writing and reading skills

Did you know that teachers are helping you develop your **writing** in at least eight ways? These are called 'assessment focuses' (AFs) and they are described here.

AF	Teacher language	This means...
1	Write imaginative, interesting and thoughtful texts	My writing is imaginative, interesting and thoughtful
2	Produce texts which are appropriate to the task, reader and purpose	I am able to write for different purposes and audiences according to the task set
3	Organise and present whole texts effectively, sequencing and structuring information, ideas and events	I can plan my writing and produce texts that sequence ideas, information and events within an appropriate structure
4	Construct paragraphs and use cohesion within and between paragraphs	I can use topic sentences and linking sentences to guide my reader through the text
5	Vary sentences for clarity, purpose and effect	I can use different types of sentences – simple, compound and complex – according to purpose and to create specific effects
6	Write with technical accuracy of syntax and punctuation in phrases, clauses and sentences	I am able to use different types of punctuation to make the meaning clear to my reader
7	Select appropriate and effective vocabulary	I can select and use a range of vocabulary, making choices according to purpose and audience
8	Use correct spelling	I can spell accurately

Reading is not just about being able to say and understand the words you see. Reading skills include the different ways you are expected to respond to a text. The seven assessment focuses for reading are:

AF	Teacher language	This means...
1	Use a range of strategies, including accurate decoding of text, to read for meaning	I can read for meaning
2	Understand, describe, select or retrieve information, events or ideas from texts and use quotations and references from texts	I can understand and pick out the appropriate quote, event or idea from a text and use PEE (Point, Evidence, Explain) to demonstrate my understanding
3	Deduce, infer or interpret information, events or ideas from texts	I can read and understand meaning that is only hinted at
4	Identify and comment on the structure and organisation of texts, including grammatical and presentational features at text level	I can identify the text type according to its presentational features and conventions. I can also comment on the writer's choice of text type to suit purpose
5	Explain and comment on the writer's use of language, including grammatical and literary features at word and sentence level	I can explain why the writer has made certain language choices (imperative verbs, emotive language, figurative language, formal/informal etc.)
6	Identify and comment on writers' purposes and viewpoints and the overall effect of a text on the reader	I can identify the writer's purpose and viewpoint and comment on how this affects the reader
7	Relate texts to their social, cultural and historical contexts and literary traditions	I can see how texts fit into their cultural and historical traditions

Reading comprehension

ABOUT THE READING TEST

The Reading Test comes in the form of two booklets – one containing the texts you will read and another with the questions and space for your answers.

You have 1 hour for the test, including 15 minutes to read the booklets and 45 minutes to answer all the questions.

Reading the texts

Read the text in the booklet. DON'T RUSH. Make sure you read the contents page; it has key information which prepares you for the types of texts you will be reading, for example *A country of colour* – a brief summary of how South Africa has changed in recent years.

DON'T RUSH!

If there are words you don't understand, read on and perhaps the paragraph will make sense anyway.

The questions

Always read the question carefully before you write. Look at the top of the page; it will tell you which section of the reading booklet you need to look at.

There are different types of questions which you will begin to recognise.

★ Some questions require a short answer, for example *who, what, when* style questions.

★ Some questions require a longer answer, for example *why, how, do you think* questions.

★ Some questions involve no writing at all, but instead you will need to circle the right answer, tick some boxes or match up ideas.

★ You might be asked to comment on why an author has used a particular word or phrase.

★ You could be asked about how a text is organised, for example pictures, subheadings, text in boxes, bold print, etc.

★ Some questions ask for your opinions and views – remember to link these to the text.

Answering the questions

After you have read the question, look across in the margin and you will see how many marks the question is worth (these usually range from 1 to 3 marks). This should help you to structure your answer. You must REFER TO THE TEXT in your answers – you can read the reading booklet as many times as you want! Although some of the questions require deep thinking, the answers will always relate to the reading booklet.

REFER TO THE TEXT

Reading between the lines

Authors don't always tell you exactly what is happening. They often give you clues to help you work it out for yourself.

> Josh cried long and deep into his hands. The lead hung from his pocket like a wilted flower and the hewed tennis ball was still wet from its last game with Spike. Had this actually happened? The smell of burnt tyres and the angry face of the driver told him it had.

(1) What was hanging from Josh's pocket?

The answer can be found in the text itself – the lead.

(2) What or who is Spike?

The text doesn't actually say, but from reading the clues (lead and chewed tennis ball) it becomes clear that Spike is a dog.

(3) What has just happened?

Again, the text doesn't actually say, but you can draw your own conclusion from the text. 'The smell of burnt tyres', 'the angry face of the driver' and Josh's distress all imply that Spike has been hit by a car.

Top tips	★ **Check how many marks each question is worth:**
	   – One mark usually means the answer is in the WORDS of the text.
	   – Two or three marks usually mean that you are being asked to work out what the author meant – to read between the lines – or to draw on your own knowledge and experience.
	 ★ **Always answer 2- or 3-mark questions with evidence or examples from the text.**
	 ★ **When a question begins *Why do you think ...?* or *How do you know ...?* you should always BACK UP YOUR ANSWER with examples from the text.**

Achieving Level 4 reading

At Level 4, you show that you can understand a range of texts and understand their ideas, themes, events and characters. You show that you are beginning to use inference and deduction to read between the lines and can bring your own experiences into your understanding. You refer to the text when explaining your views. You can find and use ideas and information from different parts of a text.

If you can do all of these, you will achieve Level 4 and possibly even Level 5!

Text 1 (Non-fiction)

Go Ape!

The following text is taken from a leaflet to advertise an outdoor adventure park called *Go Ape!*

It's not in the dictionary, but if it was, Go Ape would be described as a 'high-wire forest adventure'.

That means we build giant obstacle courses up in the trees using ladders, walkways, bridges and tunnels made of wood, rope and super-strong wire, and top it all off with the country's best zip lines (including the longest at 426 metres – check it out on You Tube).

We then kit people out with harnesses and pulleys, give them a 30-minute safety briefing and training and let them loose into the forest, free to swing through the trees. Of course, instructors are always on hand, regularly patrolling the forests.

The result is spectacular. The Go Ape experience gets the adrenalin pumping, gets people out of their comfort zones and above all (no pun intended), it's just great fun.

How safe is it? When you're 40-feet up in the air and walking across a wire the thickness of one of your fingers, you need to know you're safe. We take safety extremely seriously and we ensure everyone who comes to Go Ape knows what they're doing and has the skills to complete a course without putting themselves or anyone else in danger. Before you head out onto the course, you'll be given a half-hour safety briefing by one of our qualified instructors. Here you'll learn and try out the obstacles at low levels, and get to grips with the equipment. It's not complicated, but it's important stuff and it will give you confidence to enjoy your time up in the trees.

Guidelines for participants:
Minimum age: 10 years
Minimum height: 1.4 m (4ft 7")
Maximum weight: 130 kg (20.5 stones)
Maximum number of participants: 14 per session

Tips

★ Read the text all the way through, then reread it more slowly. If you do not understand any of the vocabulary, read on through the sentence or the paragraph and see if that helps you to understand the word.

★ When you have read it twice, think about the purpose of the text. Is it to entertain you, make you think in a certain way or give you facts and information?

★ Read all the questions before you try to answer them. Check that you understand what each question is asking you to do.

Practice questions

If you need more space for your answers use extra paper.

1 How tall do you have to be to take part in a 'Go Ape' visit?

_____

AF2

1

1 mark

2 This is an advert for *Go Ape*. Why do you think the designer chose to include photographs in the advert?

_____

AF4

2

1 mark

3 Find and copy a phrase which suggests *Go Ape* gives a real challenge to people who do not have much adventure in their lives.

_____

AF5

3

1 mark

4 Why is it important to try low obstacles first?

_____

AF3

4

1 mark

5 How long is the zip line at *Go Ape*?

_____

AF2

5

2 marks

6 Imagine you have been to *Go Ape*. Using the advert, write about your experience.

_____

_____

AF7

6

2 marks

7 List **three** ways in which *Go Ape* prepares you before you go on the high-wire forest adventure?

_____

_____

_____

AF3

7

3 marks

8 Tick **three** materials which the tunnels are made from.

Super-strong wire ☐   Wood ☐   Clay ☐

Plastic ☐   Rope ☐   Glass ☐

AF2

8

3 marks

HOW DID YOU DO? See page 63 for the answers.

Total marks ____

51

Text 2 (Non-fiction)

Interview with Valerie Bloom

Where do you get your ideas from?
Ideas come from all over. Sometimes I read something, I listen to the radio, I watch television, I listen to people talking. I eavesdrop quite a lot I'm afraid. I get ideas from that. Sometimes they just jump up and hit you over the head when you're least expecting it, which is why, wherever I go, I have a notebook, because as soon as the ideas come, I jot them down.

Why do you write poetry?
I write poems because I like to be able to say a lot in a few words and you do that with poetry. I love playing around with words, which you can do with poetry, not so much with prose: I do write prose as well, I write novels. I enjoy doing that as well. But the other thing about writing poetry is that you can write a poem and have a finished product in a very short time, so I can write a poem in the bath, I can write a poem on the train, I can write a poem in my hotel room, so I can have a book finished in a short time.

Does music influence your writing?
Music is a big influence. I came from Jamaica. In the Caribbean, the art-forms are not separate. You don't just have poetry in one section and music in another, they are all inter-related. So you would get a poem which has singing and dancing and so on and I draw on that culture when I write. A lot of my poetry draws on folk songs quite a lot and I use rap in my writing and all those musical forms that I grew up with influence my writing.

What do you like doing when you're not writing?
I like cooking, I like gardening, especially working with my bonsai tree. I get very calm and peaceful feelings working with my bonsai tree. It's very good for writing. I like playing word games. Games like Scrabble, though nobody will play with me any more. They say I make up words, but I don't really.

Who do you think of when you're writing a poem?
Mainly I'm thinking about myself. I'm thinking about what excites me, what makes me laugh, what makes me sad or whatever. If I can write for myself and the number of people who are inside me, the child, or the old person, or the man, or the boy or the girl, then I think I will reach other people. Occasionally, when I'm writing poems for performance I think about the audience and I think what they would like to do and what I can give them to do so they can become part of the poem.

Tips	★ Read the text all the way through, then reread it more slowly. If you do not understand any of the vocabulary, read on through the sentence or the paragraph and see if that helps you understand the word.
	★ When you have read it twice, think about the purpose of the text. Is it to entertain you, make you think in a certain way or give you facts and information?
	★ Read all the questions before you try to answer them. Check that you understand what each question is asking you to do.

Practice questions

If you need more space for your answers use extra paper.

1 Find and copy a phrase from the interview which explains why Valerie always takes a notebook with her wherever she goes.

_____

_____

AF3

[   ] 1

1 mark

2 Tick the box which shows the country Valerie is from.

England [   ]   China [   ]   Jamaica [   ]   Spain [   ]

AF2

[   ] 2

1 mark

3 Why is it difficult for Valerie to find people to play Scrabble with her?

_____

_____

AF2

[   ] 3

1 mark

4 This interview has been published on a website. In what other format might it be published?

_____

AF7

[   ] 4

1 mark

5 Valerie's words are written in the first person during this interview. Give another feature that shows this is an interview.

_____

_____

AF4

[   ] 5

1 mark

6 Tick **two** boxes which show what Valerie's hobbies are.

Football [   ]   Playing the flute [   ]

Cooking [   ]   Singing [   ]

Gardening [   ]   Going to the cinema [   ]

AF3

[   ] 6

2 marks

HOW DID YOU DO? See page 63 for the answers.

Total marks [   ]

Text 3 (Fiction)

Bootleg

This extract has been taken from a book called *Bootleg* by Alex Shearer. It is set in the future when the government is forcing everyone to lead healthier lives.

Chocolate addicts Smudger and Huntly watch in horror as chocolate is banned from the shops and Chocolate Troopers arrest anyone caught with sweets. In this part of the story, it has been a long time since the boys have had chocolate and they go to try and buy some from a secret chocolate seller known as a bootlegger. They are kicking a bottle around as they wait for the chocolate seller.

After a few minutes, the man closed the bonnet of his van and sauntered over to where the boys were playing.

'Having a kickabout, lads?' he asked.

'That's it,' Smudger said. It was pretty obvious what they were doing.

'Hungry work kicking a ball about,' the man continued.

Huntly and Smudger exchanged a look. They stopped kicking the bottle.

'Yes,' the man went on, 'very hungry work is kicking a ball – or even a bottle – about. Makes you long for some kind of high-energy food supplement. Something full of energy to give you a bit of a *Boost*! Something with a bit of *Fruit and Nut* in it. Makes you wonder how they cope on the rest of the *Galaxy*. Makes you wonder if they play football on *Mars*. I sometimes wonder if there's life up there in the *Milky Way*. But you'd have to be quite a *Smartie* pants to know the answer to that one.'

And having delivered this odd speech, the man returned to his van and stood by the back door, leaning on the roof, and staring up at the sky. Huntly and Smudger looked questioningly at each other. Was this him? The black marketeer? He certainly didn't look like one. Not for a moment. He seemed quite ordinary. You'd never have thought –

But yes! That was the whole idea. You'd never have suspected for a moment.

Huntly and Smudger walked over towards the van, just as casually as the man had a few seconds earlier. At their approach he wordlessly reached out, turned a handle and opened the rear doors, so that the two boys could see inside.

'Take a look, lads,' he said. 'Shop around. Whatever you fancy.'

They looked into the van. Then they gawped, with eyes like saucers and expressions of such surprise that the chocolate seller almost laughed.

There was everything in there! Every chocolate bar you could name or think of. The van was full up with Dairy Milk, Twix, Rolos, the lot.

Practice questions

If you need more space for your answers use extra paper.

1 What are Smudger and Huntly playing football with?

_____

AF2

1

1 mark

2 When the bootlegger opens the van, the author describes Huntly and Smudger's reactions as 'Then they gawped, with eyes like saucers'. What does the writer's choice of words tell you about how the boys felt when they looked into the van?

_____

_____

AF4

2

1 mark

3 Why is the man leaning on the roof and staring up at the sky? Tick the right answer.

He is looking at the sun. ☐   He is very hot. ☐

He is fixing his van. ☐   He is waiting. ☐

AF3, 4

3

1 mark

4 The man says: 'Something with a bit of _Fruit and Nut_ in it. Makes you wonder how they cope on the rest of the _Galaxy_. Makes you wonder if they play football on _Mars_.'
Why have some of the words here been put in italics?

_____

_____

AF4

4

2 marks

5 Huntly and Smudger 'looked questioningly at each other' when deciding what to do as they looked at the chocolate seller. Why do you think they do this? Tick **two** answers below.

They are nervous and worried they may get caught. ☐

They are hot and tired in the sun. ☐

They are thinking about their homework. ☐

They are not sure if they can trust the chocolate seller. ☐

AF6

5

2 marks

HOW DID YOU DO? See page 63 for the answers.

Total marks [ ]

Text 4 (Poetry)

Daddy fell into the pond

Alfred Noyes

Everyone grumbled. The sky was grey.
We had nothing to do and nothing to say.
We were nearing the end of a dismal day,
And then there seemed to be nothing beyond,
Then
Daddy fell into the pond!

And everyone's face grew merry and bright,
And Timothy danced for sheer delight.
'Give me the camera, quick, oh quick!
He's crawling out of the duckweed!' Click!

Then the gardener suddenly slapped his knee,
And doubled up, shaking silently,
And the ducks all quacked as if they were daft,
And it sounded as if the old drake laughed.
Oh, there wasn't a thing that didn't respond
When
Daddy fell into the pond!

Tips	★ Read the text all the way through, then reread it more slowly. If you do not understand any of the vocabulary, read on through the sentence or the paragraph and see if that helps you understand the word.
	★ When you have read it twice, think about the purpose of the text. Is it to entertain you, make you think in a certain way or give you facts and information?
	★ Read all the questions before you try to answer them. Check that you understand what each question is asking you to do.

Practice questions

If you need more space for your answers use extra paper.

1 What did Timothy do when Daddy fell into the pond?

_____

AF2 [ ] 1
1 mark

2 *'Give me the camera, quick, oh quick!*
He's crawling out of the duckweed!' Click!

What is happening when 'click' comes at the end of this verse?

_____

AF6 [ ] 2
1 mark

3 How is the atmosphere different in the final verse of the poem?

_____

_____

AF3,5 [ ] 3
2 marks

4 In the first verse, the author chooses to place the word 'Then' by itself. What is the effect of this?

_____

_____

AF5 [ ] 4
2 marks

5 Find and copy **three** words or phrases in the first verse which show that it was a really miserable day for everyone.

_____

_____

AF5 [ ] 5
3 marks

6 Why do you think the author included direct speech in the middle of this poem?

_____

_____

AF6 [ ] 6
2 marks

HOW DID YOU DO? See page 63 for the answers.

Total marks [ ]

57

Handwriting

Handwriting is assessed in the Longer Writing Task, so do your best to keep it neat and easy to read. You can get a maximum of three marks for handwriting, and if you follow these hints and examples, they will be easy marks to achieve!

The golden rules

- Space out words and sentences evenly.
- Write on the lines if you are using lined paper.
- Use a pen or pencil you feel comfortable with and always use an eraser to rub out mistakes.
- Keep the letters the same size.
- Write so everyone can read your writing!

Example: 1-mark handwriting

If your handwriting looks like this, you need to work on:

- joining up letters so they flow together neatly
- keeping the letters the same size
- spacing out the letters evenly. Some of these words are quite squashed!

Once upon a time. long ago there was a princess. She was the most beutiful princess in the world. Her dress sparkled as much as her charming atitude. She was the happiest prettiest person in the world.

Example: 2-mark handwriting

If your handwriting looks like this, you need to work on:

- making sure all, not just some, of the letters are joined together
- getting the ascenders (the upward strokes like *d* and *b*) to lean in the same direction.

Once upon a time, long ago there was a princess. She was the most beautiful princess in all the land. Her dress Sparkled as much as her charming attitude. She was the happiest, prettiest person in the world.

Overall, the shape and size of the letters are even and the writing is easy to read.

Example: 3-mark handwriting

If your handwriting looks like this, you're going to get top marks! The letters are all correctly formed and are evenly

Once upon a time, long ago there was a princess. She was the most beautiful princess in all the land. Her dress sparkled as much as her charming attitude. She was the happiest, prettiest person in the world.

sized and spaced. The other good thing about this handwriting is that it has its own style, so try to develop a style of your own.

Hints and Tips	★ Compare a sample of your handwriting with the ones on this page. Which one is it most like? What are you doing well? What do you need to work on to make it better? ★ Go over what needs to improve with a highlighter pen, then rewrite the same sample, making as many improvements as you can. ★ Practise a few sentences at a time, rewriting them and making improvements. ★ Try especially hard to join the letters – it really speeds up writing!

Glossary

Adjectives words that add information or description to nouns

Adverbs words that add information or description to verbs

Cause what makes something happen

Character someone in a story; what someone is like, personality

Comprehension understanding

Conclusion the end of something; the resulting idea or thought about something

Connectives words that are used to link sentences and paragraphs

Deduction the use of evidence in the text to work out what the author is telling you, to read *between* the lines

Dialogue the words spoken by characters in a story

Effect the result of something happening

Emotive appealing to the emotions and making us feel in different ways

Evidence something that proves what you think or believe

Fiction stories that are imagined, not real

Imperative verbs that give a command, e.g. *Go* or *Put*

Inference the use of your own knowledge *and* the evidence in the text to come to a conclusion about what the author means, to read *beyond* the lines

Issue a matter or subject for discussion

Logical resulting naturally

Non-fiction texts that give you information

Omission missing out

Paragraphs a number of sentences grouped together, usually linked by idea, topic, time, place or theme

Passive voice a verb form where the action is done by someone else, e.g. *it was thrown*. The 'opposite' of this is the **active voice**, where the subject of the sentence does the action, e.g. *he threw it*

Possession owning

Problem something that goes wrong

Proper noun a noun that names a person, place or organisation

Recommendation what you think should be done

Resolution how a problem is sorted out

Review look back at critically or carefully

Setting where a story takes place

Stereotype a character, usually in a fairy story or traditional tale, who has no real distinguishing characteristics, e.g. *a bad witch, a handsome prince*

Summary a short piece of writing that sums up the main points

Theme an idea that a story or poem is about

Learning objectives for Primary English

This chart shows you the objectives required to achieve Level 4 in English.

Strand	Year 5	Year 6
Word structure and spelling	• Spell words with unstressed vowels (*doctor*, *around*) • Know and use prefixes and suffixes like *im-*, *-ir-*, *-cian* • Group and classify words by their spelling patterns and their meanings	• Spell familiar words correctly; use a range of strategies to spell difficult or unfamiliar words • Edit, proofread and correct spelling in your own work, on paper and on screen
Understand and interpret texts	• Make notes on and use evidence from across a text • Infer writers' perspectives • Compare different types of texts; identify their structure • Know that a word can mean different things in different contexts • Explore how writers use language to create comic and dramatic effects	• Quickly decide on a text's value, quality or usefulness • Understand a text's themes, causes and points of view • Understand how writers use different structures to create an impact • Explore how word meanings change when used in different contexts • Recognise rhetorical devices used to persuade and mislead
Engage with and respond to texts	• Reflect on reading habits and plan your own reading goals • Know different ways to explore the meaning of texts • Compare how a theme is presented in poetry, prose and other media	• Read widely; discuss your own reading with others • Read longer texts • Compare how writers from different times and places present experiences and use language
Create and shape texts	• Reflect on your own writing; edit and improve it • Experiment with different forms and styles when writing stories, non-fiction and poetry • Use direct and reported speech, action and selection of detail to vary pace and viewpoint • Create multi-layered texts, including use of hyperlinks and linked web pages	• Set yourself challenges to extend achievement in writing • Use different techniques to engage and entertain the reader in narrative and non-narrative • Select words and language, drawing on your knowledge of literary features • Integrate words, images and sounds imaginatively for different purposes
Text structure and organisation	• Experiment with the order of sections and paragraphs to achieve different effects • Change the order of material within a paragraph, moving the topic sentence	• Use varied structures to shape and organise text coherently • Use paragraphs to achieve pace and emphasis
Sentence structure and punctuation	• Adapt sentence construction to different text types and readers • Punctuate sentences accurately, including using speech marks and apostrophes	• Express meanings, including hypothesis, speculation and supposition, by constructing sentences in varied ways • Use punctuation to clarify meaning in complex sentences
Presentation	• Adapt handwriting for specific purposes • Make informed choices about which ICT program to use for different purposes	• Use appropriate handwriting styles for different purposes • Select from a wide range of ICT programs to present text effectively and communicate information and ideas

Answers

Page 10 – Recount: Challenge
First, Next, Then, After, Finally

Page 11 – Recount: Example answer 1
Monday: Went to audition for school play. It's called The Lost Boys. We all went to the hall after school but not many boys came – Miss Jenkins was a bit cross. We'd to stand at the front one at a time and read a poem that Miss Jenkins gave to us. My voice shook! Aargh! But I got the part of the Nanny, though really wanted to be Wendy. Carly got Wendy. She's such a show-off. First rehearsal is lunch time tomorrow. I haven't got lots of lines to learn so that is good. Can't wait because I'm going to be a famous actor when I grow up!

Page 13 – Instructions and procedures:
Example answer 2
Getting dressed

What you need	What you do
Pants Socks T-shirt Trousers Sweatshirt Trainers	First put on the pants. These are small and white with three holes in them. Put your legs through the two smaller holes. Next put on the socks. There are two of these. They are long, grey tubes. Put one on each foot. Then put on the T-shirt. It goes over your head and has two holes for your arms. Put on the trousers. These are also grey but are much bigger than the socks. They go over the pants and socks. Now put on the sweatshirt over the T-shirt. It is blue and has a badge on the front. Finally put on the trainers. These are white and go on each foot. You will need to fasten the Velcro strips. Now you will look just like all the other pupils – apart from your green hair.

Page 14 – Non-chronological report:
Challenge
(Sample answer) Introduction, Appearance, Food, Habitat, Breeding

Page 15 – Non-chronological report:
Example answer 2
The Mintosaurus
Here you can see the newly discovered fossil of the Mintosaurus dinosaur.
This fossil was found by Sir Humbert Bumbert in South America in December 2008.
Amazing facts!
- *Length – 105 metres from nose to the tip of its tail.*
- *Height – 2 metres tall.*

- *Appearance – Mintosaurus had two short front legs and two powerful back legs. The front legs were short so it could bend down to graze. The back legs were strong to help it reach up to get leaves at the tops of trees. It had spines running down its back from the tip of its nose to the tip of its tail.*
- *Food – The Mintosaurus dinosaurs were herbivores. They ate the leaves of trees and also grazed on grass.*
- *Habitat – Mintosaurus has only been found in the jungles of South America.*
- *Did you know? The Mintosaurus dinosaur has been extinct for more than a million years!*

Page 17 – Explanation: Example answer 2
Dear Parents,
I am writing to tell you about a new type of lunch box that our class has invented. I hope it will make lunch times easier for your child.
The lunch box is made from recycled card, which means it is a greener box than the plastic ones most pupils use. It is split into four sections which open one after the other. This means your child will be able to eat the food in the right order. It also means that your child cannot just eat the bits they like!
There is one section for sandwiches. This opens first. When the sandwich section is empty, a spring goes off that opens the second section. This contains a drink. Next, the vegetable section opens. When the vegetable section is empty, the last section will open and your child can eat their fruit.
Using the new lunch box will help your child to eat a healthy meal at lunch time.
Yours sincerely,
Mr Andrews
Class 6A

Page 19 – Discussion: Example answer 2

Mobile phones should be allowed	Mobile phones should not be allowed
• Children can contact their friends • Parents can contact their children • Mobile phones are good fun • There are too many school rules already	• Children are already with their friends and don't need a phone to contact them • Parents can phone the school if they need to contact their children • They disrupt lessons • They cause jealousy about whose is the best phone

Page 20 – Persuasion: Challenge
have been offered, has been proven, should be eaten

Page 21 – Persuasion: Example answer 2
Football Stars Wanted!
Hill Street School Needs You!
Can you kick a football?
Can you run, tackle and dribble?
Do you want to learn how to play football?
Football is fun. You can make friends and keep fit too.

Hill Street School needs new players. Could you be one?
Try-outs
When – Thursday 12th September
Where – School playing field
Time – 3.30 p.m.
So Stop being a Couch Potato!
Come and be a Football Star!

Page 26 – Setting, characters and theme: Challenge 1

First extract: movement – strode; character – dangerous
Second extract: movement – stood straight and tall

Page 28 – Setting, characters and theme: Challenge 2

Lost and found

Beginning – Introduce one main character; establish setting
Build-up – Story gets going; character does something normal
Problem – Character finds or loses something or someone
Resolution – Lost thing/person is returned
Found thing/person not quite what it had seemed
Ending – Everything OK. Characters reflect on events

Wishing or wanting

Beginning – Introduce one main character; establish setting
Identify – What main character is wishing for or wanting
Build-up – Character goes in search of their wish
Problem – Character is stopped from getting what they want, often by another character
Resolution – Main character gets what he or she wanted
Ending – Character reflects on whether getting their wish was worth it

Page 29 – Dialogue: Challenge

1. surly, bad-tempered; 2. angry;
3. very worried, concerned or afraid;
4. frightened or angry

Page 35 – Grammar: Challenge 4

Simple sentence – He didn't look back.
Compound sentence – Halfway into his voyage home, he could contain himself no longer and he opened the locket.
Complex sentence – He set sail into the night, delighted with his daring exploits and laughing with excitement at the thought of the riches he knew would be his.

Page 36 – Grammar: Challenge

Hope put her coat as well as her scarf on. Next she put on her boots. Then her friends came round. Eventually they went to the park.

Page 38 – Grammar: Challenge

Mr Walsh was having an awful day. It was windy and wet so everybody was inside for lunch time. The children were behaving like wild animals and the classroom looked like a zoo.

Page 40 Punctuation: Practice question

The ship had been becalmed before but never for so long. Some of the men lay about the decks that baked in the heat. Others stayed below hoping for cooler air, but the smell of so many men in a small space soon sent them on deck again. 'Was that a breath of wind?' asked the first mate hopefully.
'Perhaps it was,' said Cap'n Jake, 'I think you're right. All hand to the sails!' he cried, his voice reaching all through the tiny ship. Men, women and children went scurrying aloft.
Give yourself an extra mark if you remembered to start a new speaker on a new line!

Page 42 – Vocabulary: Challenge 1

(Sample answers)
1. This is an *EXCITING* story.
2. The train had *VIVID* purple doors.
3. After the race his face was *COMPLETELY SCARLET*.
4. Mrs Lane is *LIVID*.
5. The tree had *ENORMOUS* flowers on its branches.

Page 42 – Vocabulary: Challenge 2

dangerously, angrily

Page 43 – Vocabulary: Practice questions 1

(Sample answers)
1. He *suddenly* banged the book onto the table.
2. 'You look out!' he whispered *menacingly*.
3. The monkeys climbed *rapidly* from branch to branch.
4. 'It wasn't me!' she said *firmly*.

Page 43 – Vocabulary: Practice questions 2

(Sample answers)
1. Hordes of menacing monkeys *clambered* through the high treetops.
2. The proud princess *strode* along the streets of cheering crowds.
3. She *placed* the china cups carefully in the basket.
4. The thief *scrambled* through the broken attic window.

Page 44 – Spelling: Practice question

foxes, roads, bunches, wishes, sounds, lives, taxes, trees, drinks, pirates, houses, donkeys, flies, buses

Page 45 – Spelling: Challenge

Short vowel sound: bin, chat, flutter, wet, dot

Long vowel sound: line, paper, choose, reign, meet, light, float

Page 45 – Spelling: Quick challenge

Verb	Past tense	Present tense	Future tense
To fit	I fitted I have fitted I was fitting	I fit I am fitting	I will fit
To move	I moved I have moved I was moving	I move I am moving	I will move
To clap	I clapped I have clapped I was clapping	I clap I am clapping	I will clap
To keep	I kept I have kept I was keeping	I keep I am keeping	I will keep
To swim	I swam I have swum I was swimming	I swim I am swimming	I will swim
To fly	I flew I have flown I was flying	I fly I am flying	I will fly
To produce	I produced I have produced I was producing	I produce I am producing	I will produce
To try	I tried I have tried I was trying	I try I am trying	I will try
To pursue	I pursued I have pursued I was pursuing	I pursue I am pursuing	I will pursue

Page 51 – Text 1 (Non-fiction): Go Ape!
Practice questions

1. 1.4 m (4ft 7")
2. To persuade you to go, to let you see how it really is, to bring the experience to life.
3. Any one of the following:
   'The Go Ape experience gets the adrenalin pumping.'
   'Gets people out of their comfort zones.'
   'It's just great fun.'
4. It gives people confidence so they can enjoy their adventure in the trees.
5. 426 metres.
6. **Either** 1 mark for an expression such as 'Wow, amazing' and 1 mark for a reference to the tunnels, zip line, trees, ladders, walkways, bridges **or** 1 mark for an expression such as 'Arghhh, so scary' and 1 mark for a reference to the tunnels, zip line, trees, ladders, walkways, bridges.
7. A 30-minute safety training session, try out obstacles at low levels, try out/get used to the equipment.
8. Wood, rope and super-strong wire,
   3 correct = 3 marks, 2 correct = 2 marks and
   1 correct = 1 mark

Page 53 – Text 2 (Non-fiction): Interview with Valerie Bloom
Practice questions

1. 'Sometimes they just jump up and hit you over the head when you're least expecting it.'
2. Jamaica.
3. Because people say that she makes up words.
4. One of: newspaper, magazine.
5. Any one of: questions and answers, questions in bold, the questions and answers are given directly without using 'He said' or 'She replied' etc.
6. Cooking and gardening. *(1 mark for each)*

Page 55 – Text 3 (Fiction): Bootleg
Practice questions

1. A bottle.
2. The boys are amazed. Instead of saying 'the boys are amazed' the author says that their eyes were like saucers, meaning they opened them really wide with excitement.
3. He is waiting.
4. These are the names of chocolates and sweets. *(1 mark)* As he is a bootlegger/secret chocolate seller he doesn't want to say the word 'chocolate', so he is dropping hints/clues. *(1 mark)*
5. They are nervous and worried they may get caught. They are not sure if they can trust the chocolate seller.

Page 57 – Text 4 (Poetry): Daddy fell into the pond
Practice questions

1. He danced with sheer delight (and asked for the camera).
2. (Timothy) is taking a photograph/photo being taken.
3. The atmosphere changes because everybody comes alive and is happier. *(1 mark)* For example, the children and the gardener dance, the ducks quack and the old drake laughs. *(1 mark for an example of how the people change)*
4. Placing the word 'Then' by itself marks a change in the tone of the poem. *(1 mark)* It emphasises how exciting it was when Daddy fell in. The word 'Then' **introduces** that something exciting happened and it also **separates** the dull mood from the exciting mood. *(1 mark)*
5. Any three of the following:
   'Everyone grumbled.'
   'The sky was grey.'
   'We had nothing to do and nothing to say.'
   'We were nearing the end of a dismal day.'
   'And then there seemed to be nothing beyond,'
6. Direct speech adds to the excitement of the poem. *(1 mark)* It helps to bring the poem to life/helps you to imagine the scene. *(1 mark)*